Melodic Chords for Guitar Vol. I

BY DAVID BLOOM

Table of Contents

David Bloom is director of the nationally recognized **Bloom School of Jazz** in Chicago, which he founded in 1975. Mr. Bloom taught at Northwestern University and Roosevelt University and instructed the United States Air Force Reserve Band.

A noted lecturer and writer, he is the author of instructional books including *Major Blues for Guitar; Minor Blues for Guitar; The II V I Book; Melodic Chords for Guitar; The Question and Answer Book; Melodic Linkage, Rhythms Around the Body;* and *Ear Training Sight Singing*.

Mr. Bloom has lectured to student groups, including the American Institute of Graphic Artists, on the synergy and cooperation found in jazz groups. His book reviews and articles have appeared in the *Chicago Tribune* and numerous music publications.

Mr. Bloom began studying guitar at age nine. He later studied with blues-guitar icon Buddy Guy, noted jazz guitarist Reggie Boyd, and flute luminaries Joe Kainz and Chris Hinze before attending the renowned Berklee School of Music. From 1971 to 1980 he led his own band, for which he composed, arranged and played guitar and flute. A composer and arranger, Mr. Bloom has collaborated with noted Chicago conductor and arranger Cliff Colnot on "Duende," a critically acclaimed CD of original band jazz.

The Bloom School of Jazz

The mission of the Bloom School of Jazz is to perpetuate and promote the legacy of extreme individuality, unbridled imagination and deep feeling left us by the jazz masters.

The Bloom School of Jazz was established in 1975 by David Bloom. His original and innovative teaching methodology transcends a traditional approach to music, elevating music teaching to a study of universal human language. His teaching concepts have helped thousands of students - from beginners to professional musicians - make compelling and individualistic musical statements. The goal of the Bloom School is to seek and promote the development of each student's unique expression.

Acknowledgments

I would like to thank my mother for unending support and encouragement, Peter Lerner for his contributions to the book, Pat Fleming, Stu Greenspan and Steve Ramsdell for their helpful critiques, Reynaldo Certain for final layout, photography and graphic design, Tom Stern for copy editing and Lee Metcalf for music editing.

Fire and Form Series

Fire and Form symbolize the two basic materials in any art form. Fire represents personal expression. Form is the structural design in any artistic statement.

Great art is an expression of individuality. Creative freedom, not mere imitative slavery, requires each person to find his/her own voice. Creating one's personal statement is the ultimate artistic endeavor. In order to make this unique statement, one must first master their craft. A serious artist must have both something to say and the means with which to say it.

Any musician who wills it can become a competent jazz player. The jazz artist must understand and be able to control the material which will form the design for his/her personal statement of emotions. Jazz improvisation is the celebration of the moment through the spontaneous musical expression of the gamut of human emotions. However, it is not sufficient for a jazz musician to only express emotion without direction. In composition or improvisation, it is not enough just to create musical ideas; they must be developed and go somewhere.

This series is designed to show the artist how to go anywhere in a specific way. With this series we transcend the limitations of idiom and style, to give the artist creative freedom using the universe of musical possibilities available in Western harmony.

The basic material for all Western music is the same (the chromatic scale). Style is the artist's choice.

The **Fire and Form Series** does not deal with the presentation of different styles. It deals with musical relationships and possibilities. The style and specific use of the material is the prerogative of the player.

In this series, hearing the material has equal importance with playing the music. All music is sound. It must be heard, either as an active listener or as an active creator. The active musical creator must be able to hear a sound, either from an outside source or in his/her head, and then be able to sing, write, or play that sound. Music that is played or written without being heard first is merely chance music, in which the player does not have control of his statement. Instead of the desired vivid articulate and expressive musical statement, the player is only producing sounds.

Each book in this series can be learned in three to four months, giving serious students a new vocabulary and direction in their quest for self-expression through music.

Practice Procedure

I. You must know exactly what you're going to do BEFORE you start each exercise.

II. Practice sessions must be goal oriented.

III. Cleanliness in execution is imperative.

IV. Gaining authority should be the goal of practice.

V. Strict rhythm must always be maintained:
- a) Strict realization of rhythmic values
- b) Strict tempo maintenance

VI. Use the entire dynamic range.

VII. Never practice longer than concentration can be maintained. To practice sloppily is not effective practice. It also shows a disrespect for one's abilities and potential.

VIII. Practice with a tape recorder to evaluate what you have achieved in each practice session. Listen back to the tape to hear how precise you were in your practicing. Did you achieve the QUALITY OF EXECUTION you were looking for?

IX. You must learn to ENJOY YOUR PRACTICING. Take pride in the intensification and focus of your being. If it is a chore, proper relaxation and musicality will not happen.

X. If you make or accept mistakes in execution, you are NOT practicing effectively.

Introduction

Why was this book written?

This book was written to fulfill two basic functions. The first is to show intermediate-level guitarists how they can create more interest and direction if they gain awareness, control, and accountability for the melodies generated by their specific chord choices. **Melodic Chords for Guitar Vol. I** gives the serious guitarist the tools to play the same chord progression in numerous ways, creating a wide variety of melodies. The book demonstrates how to play chords differently, melodically, and in one's own way every time they're played.

The second is to equip players with an extensive vocabulary of **melodic chords** that include every possible tone in the top voice. This palette of **melodic chord** colors provides the serious guitarist with unending possible mixtures of chords that can be used for accompaniment (comping), chord melody, chord soloing, and composition. As each chord has at least seven melodic chord tone possibilities, then melodically connecting two chords will yield over 49 melodic connections using numerous voicings. The melodic possibilities are staggering.

What is melody?

Melody is a succession of pitches that can be constructed with the same or different rhythms. It can move up, down, or stay on the same note. It's one of the most important elements of music. Melody is the singing quality of music, and its construction makes one song memorable and another not.

What is a melodic chord?

All chords become **melodic chords** when played in succession because the notes at the top of the chords create a melody. For our purposes, I'll define a **melodic chord** as any chord that is chosen for both the chord type (Ma7, Dom7, etc.) and the note that is the highest pitched voice.

Chord melody

The complete musician must be able to render any type of chord quality: major, minor, etc., with all chord tones, extensions, and alterations in the top voice. It's obvious that to play a song, one must be able to play the melody. The ability to simultaneously play the melody and the indicated chord is called "chord melody." Guitar players must know the melody and the chords and be able to play them together.

Comping

Many musicians don't think about melody when they are accompanying (comping) someone with chords. This becomes a tremendous oversight because when a chord progression is played, a melody will occur whether one is aware of it or not. The question then becomes, what kind of melody will it be - one with an interesting melodic shape that complements the soloist or one that lacks direction and isn't responsive?

Chord knowledge - functionality vs. artistry

When most guitarists learn chords, it's usually to play a song. They will sing the melody and play the same chords (position and fingering) every time. For them, being correct and functional is often more important than playing a fresher chord choice. One of the goals great jazz guitarists have is to vary their interpretation of tunes, playing the same chord types a different way every time they're played. Similarly, many advanced blues, pop, rock, or folk musicians have made the music sound fresh and unique by increasing their chord vocabulary.

Chord colors

The greatest musicians have referred to harmony as color. Harmony can create all the hues and tints that one finds in nature. The only difference is that you hear it instead of seeing it. For those musicians who want to be able to "paint" with a full range of colors, it is critical to have a full spectrum of chords. Every chord played creates a certain feeling in the listener as well as in the musician. In order to give the listener a kaleidoscopic experience of emotions, the serious musician must have a complete and extensive chord vocabulary or "harmonic palette" and be able to connect the chords in a melodic way. These sonic colors can be used to express a full range of emotional gestures.

Voicings

There are many ways to play the same type of chord. The placement of the notes in a chord, from the bottom to the top, is called a chord voicing. Some voicings have a sharp dissonant sound while others have a smooth consonant sound. Some voicings use a few notes close to each other while others use many notes and extended range. Each chord voicing has a certain character, and often progressions use chords of the same character. In this book we have used a wide variety of chord voicings. In some progressions we have used chords of similar character, while in others we have mixed up the voicings. After you're done learning these chords, your own taste will determine which ones you use.

How to use this book

There are many ways to use this book. The pace at which you cover this material is not important, but it is critical that you memorize one complete progression before proceeding to the next. Serious, intermediate players will be able to competently learn all the material in this book in approximately three months. The criteria for excellence include being able to play each progression with clean execution, good time, and extreme dynamic contrast. As you progress, each new page will get a little easier, and after two or three pages are successfully memorized, things will move faster. As you start mastering each progression start to mix and combine the chords. In this way you will be able to play the same chord progression a myriad of ways, making it your own.

Procedure for development of the execution of chords

1. Place all of the fingers specified by the diagrams. In this book I have given specific fingerings for chords, but you can fret the notes with whatever fingering is comfortable.

2. Play each string that's indicated individually to make sure each note is ringing with a clear tone, without buzzing or muting by another finger.

3. After you can individually play all the notes cleanly, play them all together, strum them, or pluck them.

4. After you can play all the notes in a chord simultaneously, try to play the next chord. Do the same procedure for each chord.

5. To develop strong chord execution each finger should move to the next note by the closest path. Keep fingers close to the fret board and slide up or down the neck to the next note if the same finger and string is used.

6. After you can cleanly play through this progression, you're ready to move to the next progression.

Enharmonic names

Many of the chords shown in this book have multiple names. The names given to chords are determined by the function of the chord within the chord progression. One name will make sense in one chord progression but will make no sense in another. The context is very important. For example, C#o7 in one progression will be named A7b9 in another, or Cmi6, depending on the context, can be called Ami7b5.

Voice-leading

Very simply, the term "voice-leading" describes the way each note of a chord moves to the notes of the next chord. Smooth voice-leading dictates that the notes that are common between two chords remain the same while the others move to the closest chord tone of the next chord. For example, when moving from CMa7 (C-E-G-B) to F Ma7 (F-A-C-E) we notice that the notes C and E are common to both chords. To achieve smooth voice-leading the C and E will stay where they are and the B and G will move to A and F respectively. **Melodic Chords for Guitar Vol. I** focuses on melodic movement and chord quality. In Volume II, bass movement and more internal voice-leading will be covered.

To Reggie Boyd, whose musical brilliance and unbridled spirit convinced me that I could learn to play jazz.

SECTION I

APPLICATION OF MELODIC CHORDS
TO II-V-I PROGRESSIONS

We begin with the II-V-I chord progression because it's one of the most common, and it demonstrates the subdominant to dominant to tonic harmonic movement. This section illustrates **melodic chord** movement of common-tones, 2nds, 3rds, 4ths, and combinations of the previously named intervals.

On page 2 and 3 are common-tone **melodic chord** resolutions using each available chord tone in the II-V-I progression in C major. In the first II-V-I, the note C is in the melody for each chord. C is the 7th of D Mi11, the sus4th of G7, and the root of C major. In the second example the note D is the root of the Dmi7, the 5th of G7, and the 9th of CMa7. Listen as you play the chords to hear how the note D actually sounds like it's changing with each chord played. Even though we know that the note D is not actually changing, the function of the note is. In one chord D can be the root. In the next chord D can be the b9 and so on and so on. These melodic connections and resolutions dramatically demonstrate the power and color of a common-tone melody-harmony relationship. It's tantamount to coupling the past, present, and future. Any good story does exactly that.

The next **melodic chord** connections, on pages 4, 5, 6, and 7, are by 2nds. Most scales are built with major- and minor-second intervals. In addition they are the most commonly used intervals in the melodies of most tunes. It's comparatively easy to sing melodies that move up and down the scale. You will note that the resolution by 2nds is very smooth and satisfying to the ear. The first example on page 6 begins with a Dmi7 chord with C in the melody. Then we move to G7 with C# in the melody and finally to CMa9 with D in the melody. The top note of each chord or melody note is ascending by 2nds. In the second example on the same line we ascend by 2nds starting on the note D. On page 5, we again ascend by 2nds, but this time the II-V-I's are in C minor. On pages 6 and 7, we descend by 2nds in C major and C minor.

On pages 8-11, the **melodic chord** resolution is by major and minor 3rds. 3rds are very important intervals because in Western harmony, chords are built using 3rds. Whether a C major triad C-E-G is built, or a C13 (C-E-G-Bb-D-F-A), the interval of the third is the basis of chord construction. As you play these progressions you'll notice that the melodies created by the **melodic chords** are triads. On page 8 the melody created by the three chords of the first example spells a C major triad.

On pages 12-15, the **melodic chord** resolution is by 4ths. The 4th interval represents the most common harmonic movement in Western harmony. The II-V-I (Dmi7 to G7 to CMa7), one of the most common progressions, moves by 4th intervals.

On pages 16-23, ascending and descending 2rds, 3rds, and 4ths are combined to create some interesting melodic motion.

I have used many of these chord forms repeatedly, in a desire to help you burn them in. You can substitute any of these with chords from the chord dictionary.

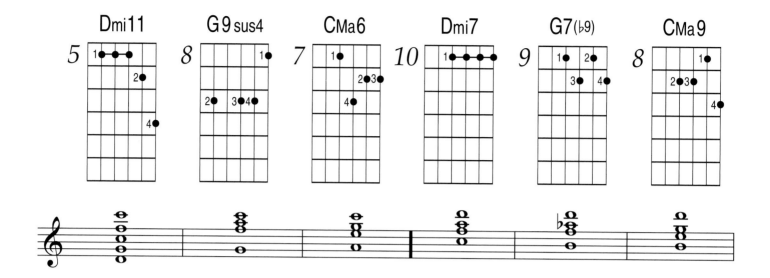

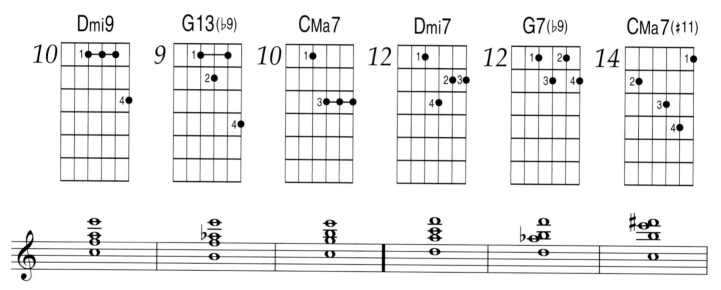

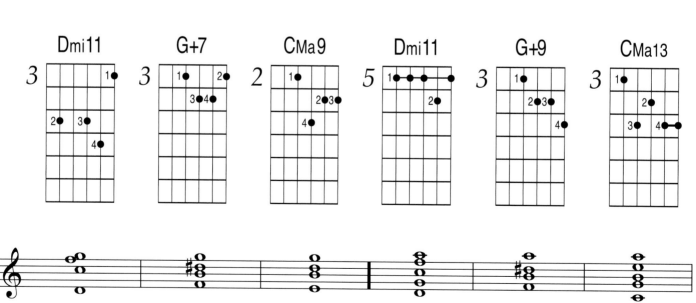

MINOR II-V-I
(CONTINUED)

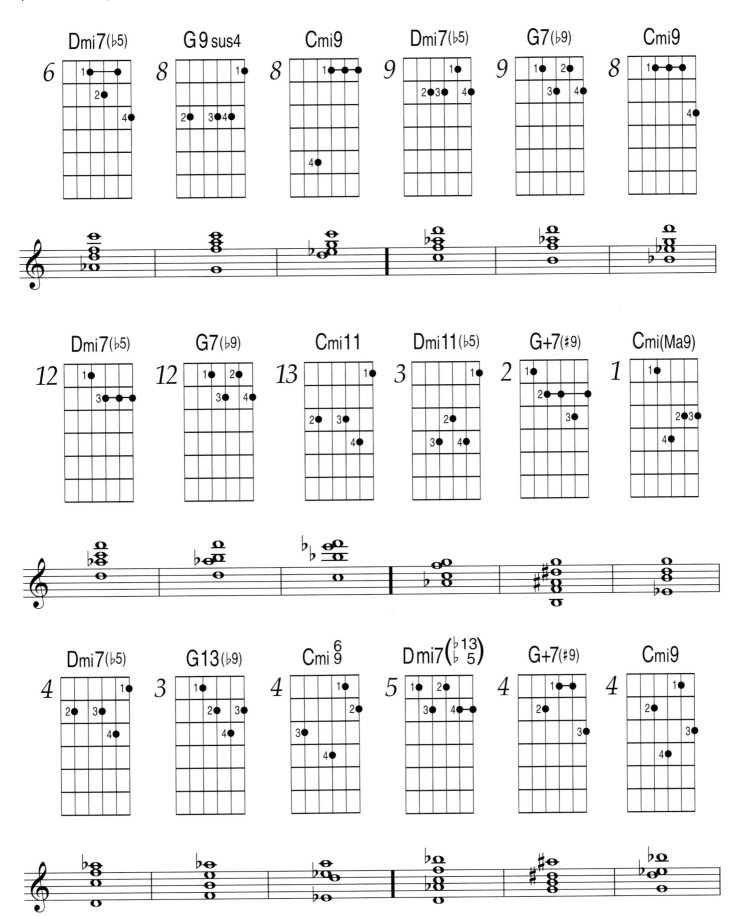

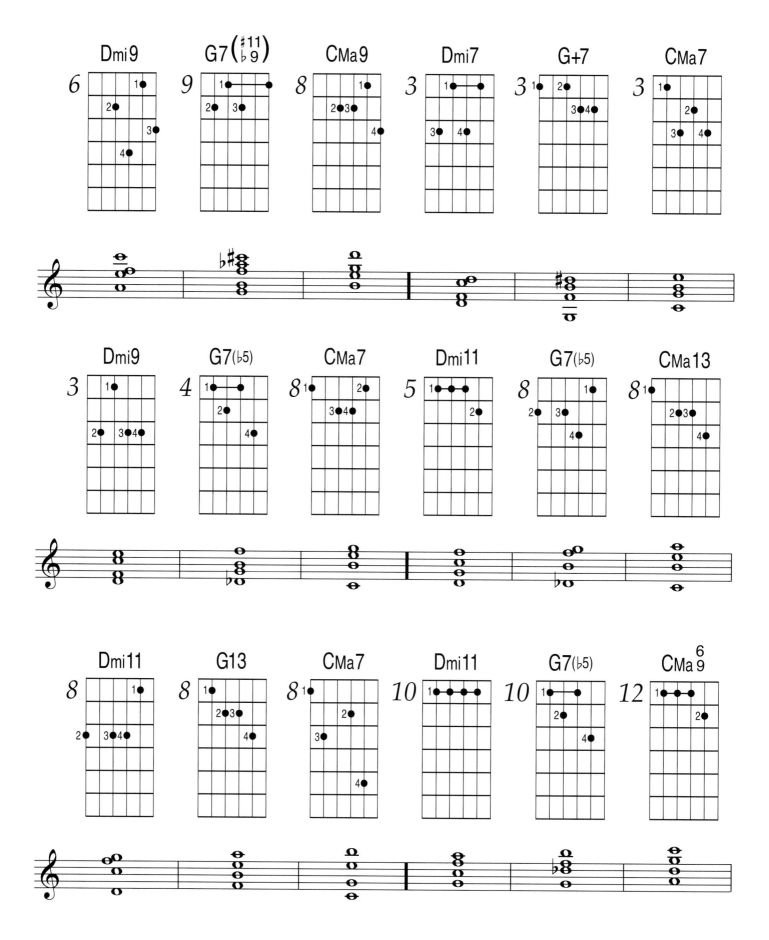

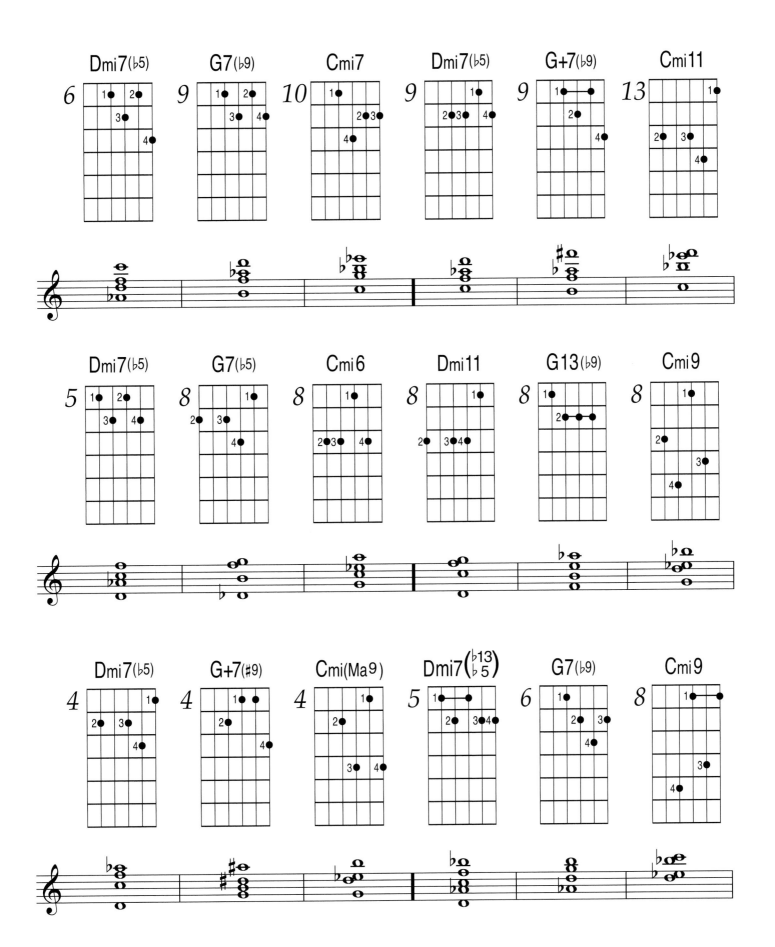

MAJOR II-V-I

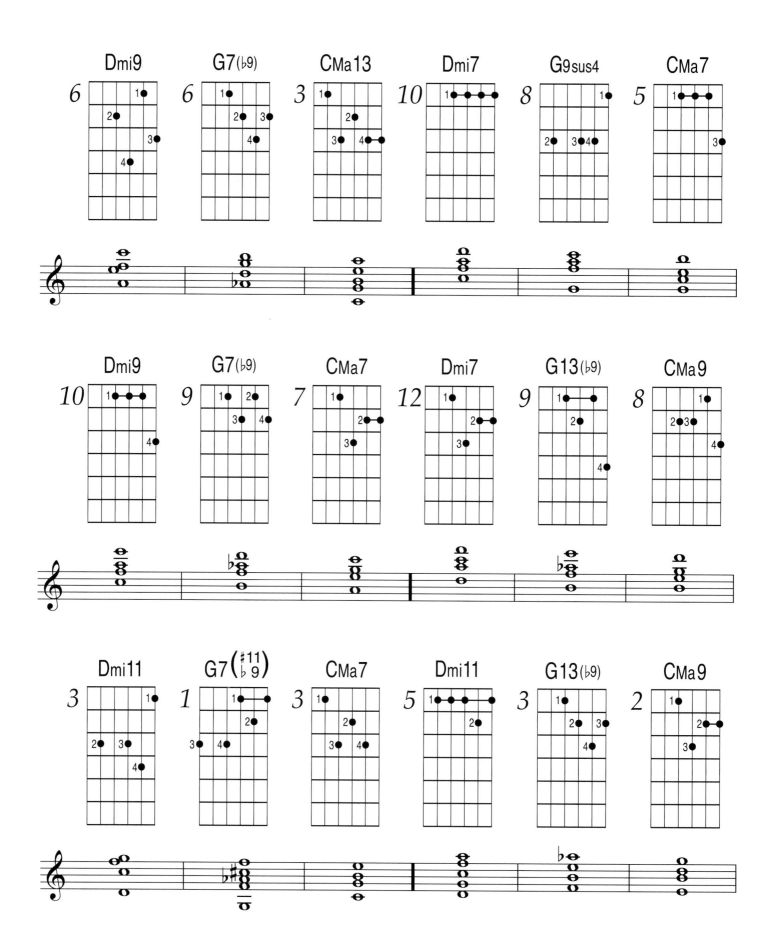

MINOR II-V-I

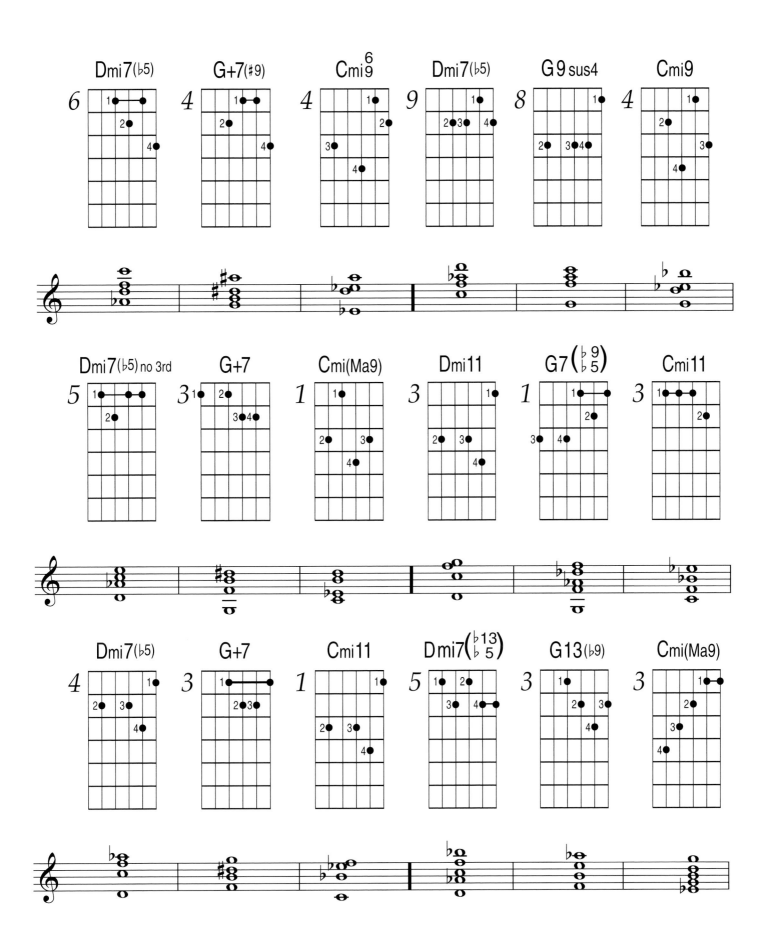

MAJOR II-V-I

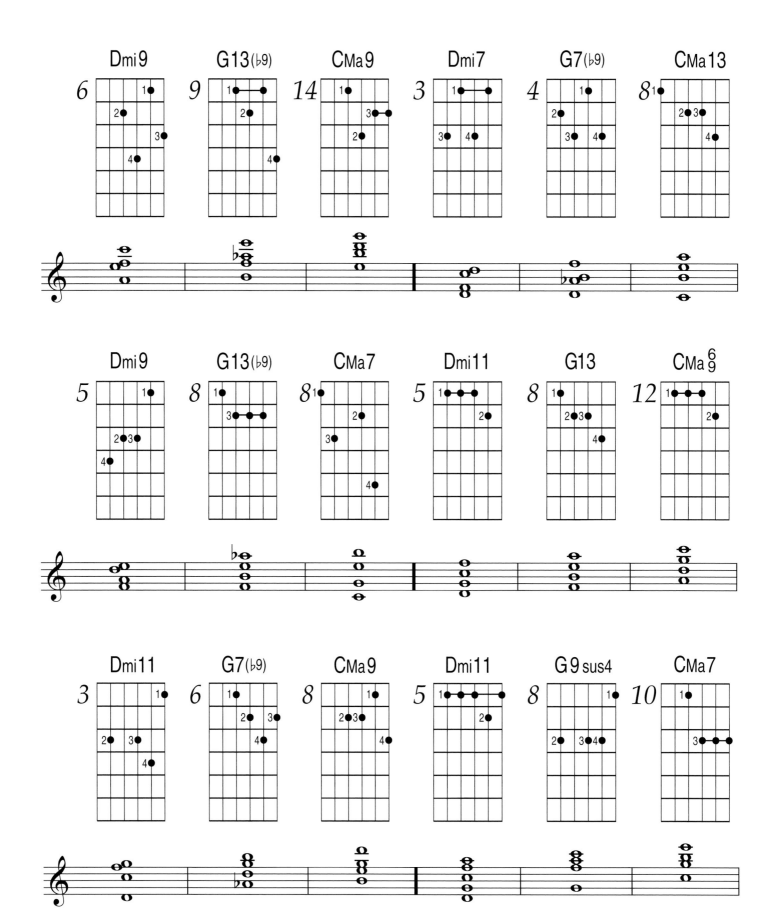

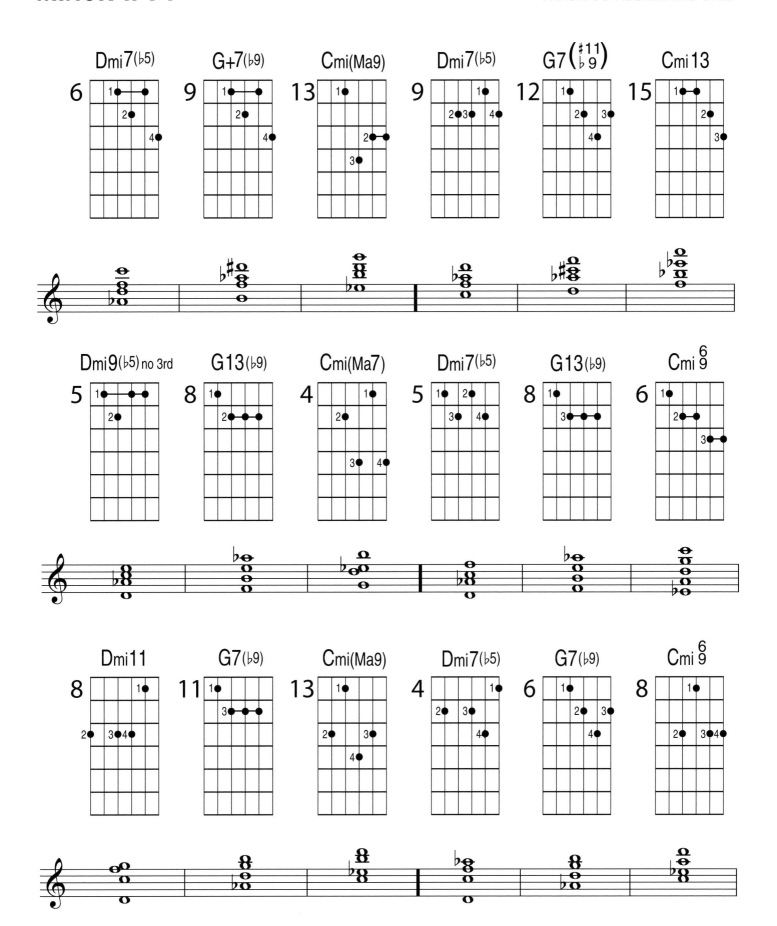

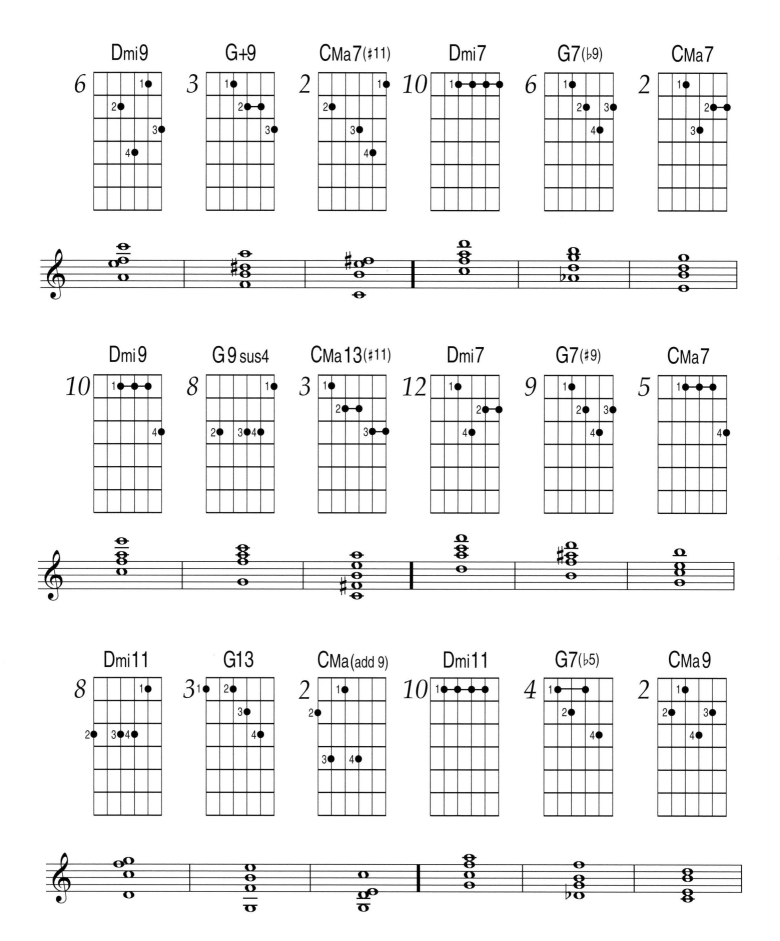

MINOR II-V-I

TRACK 11 / DESCENDING 3rds

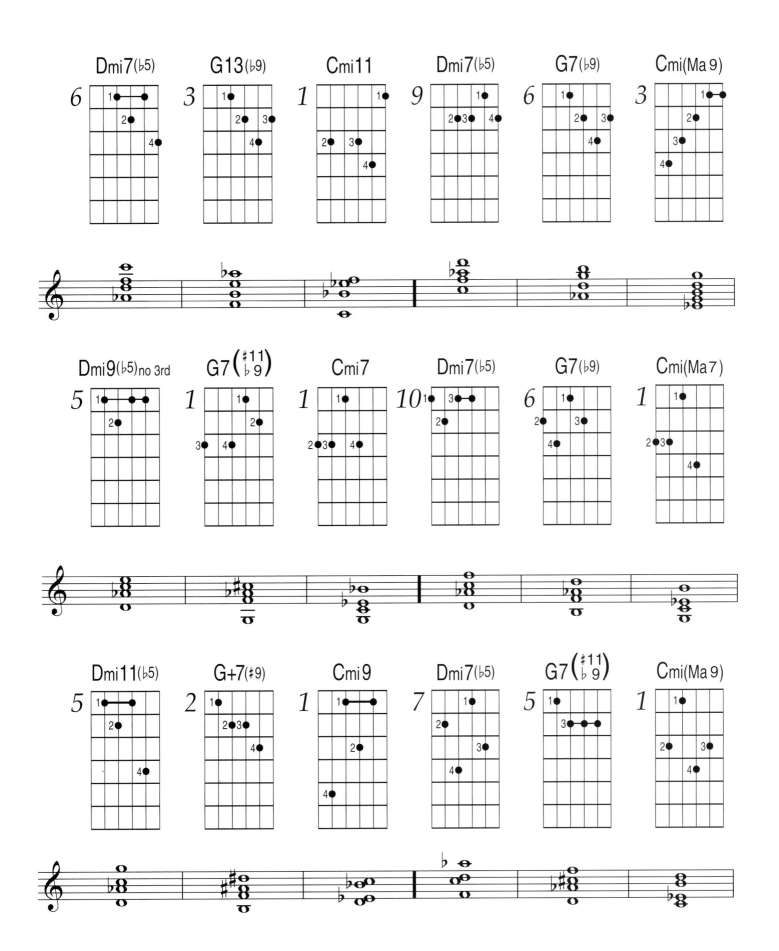

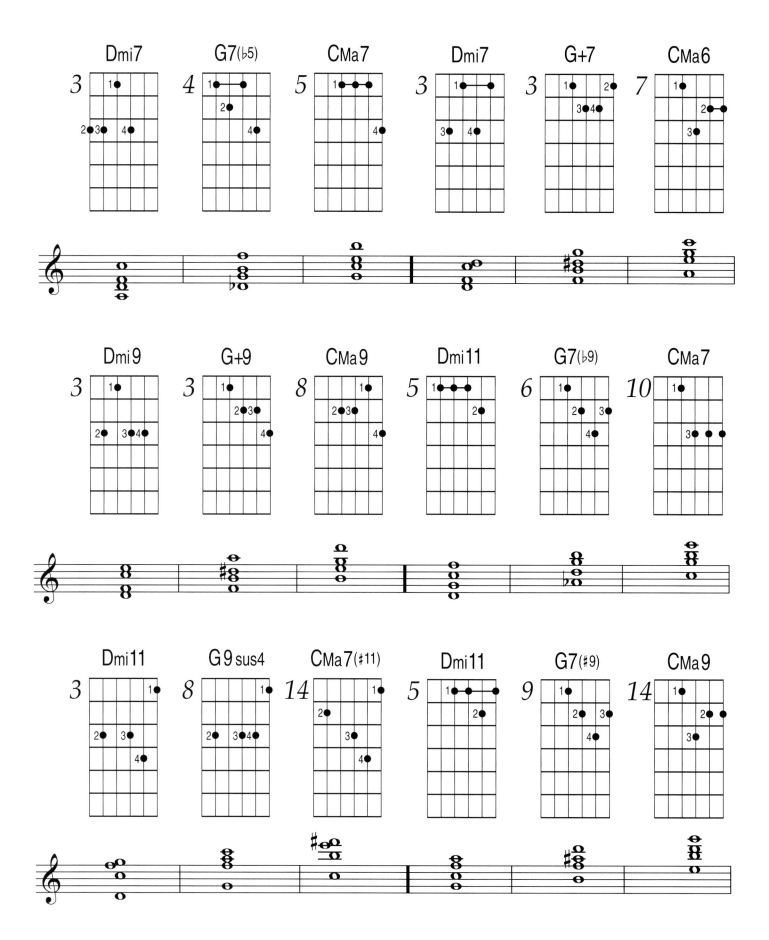

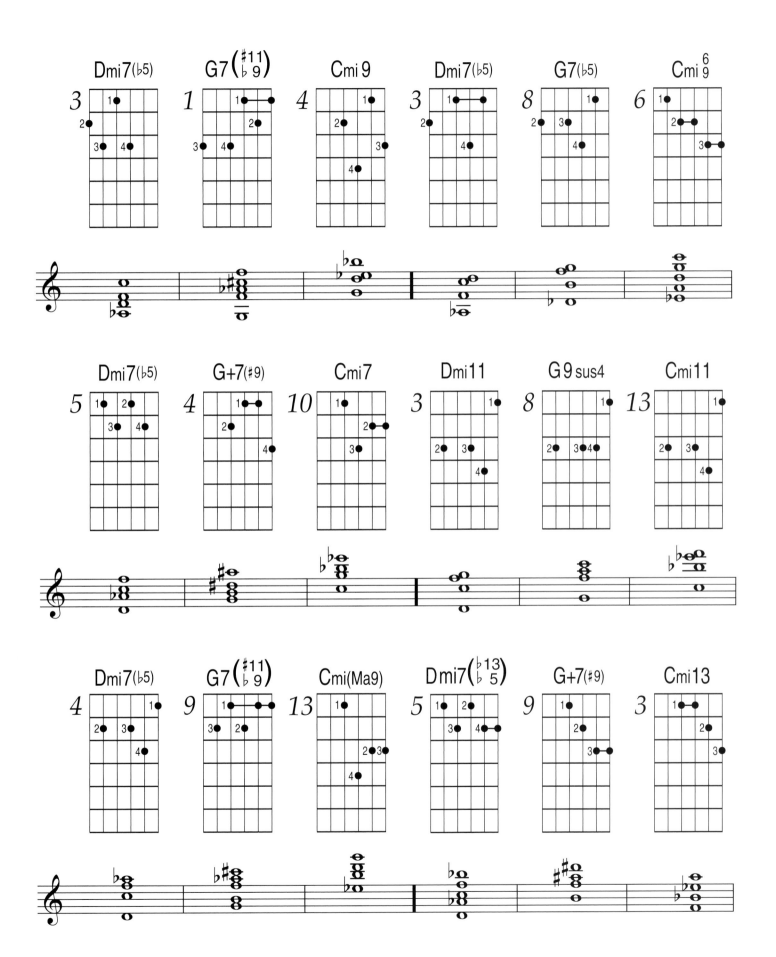

MAJOR II-V-I

TRACK 14 / DESCENDING 4ths

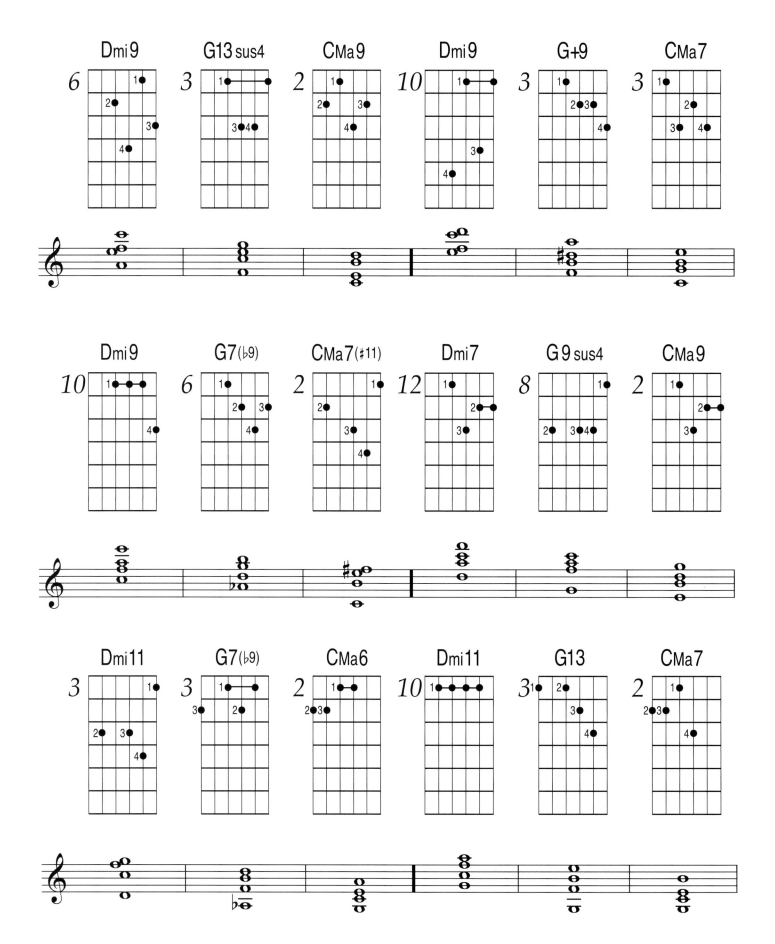

-14-

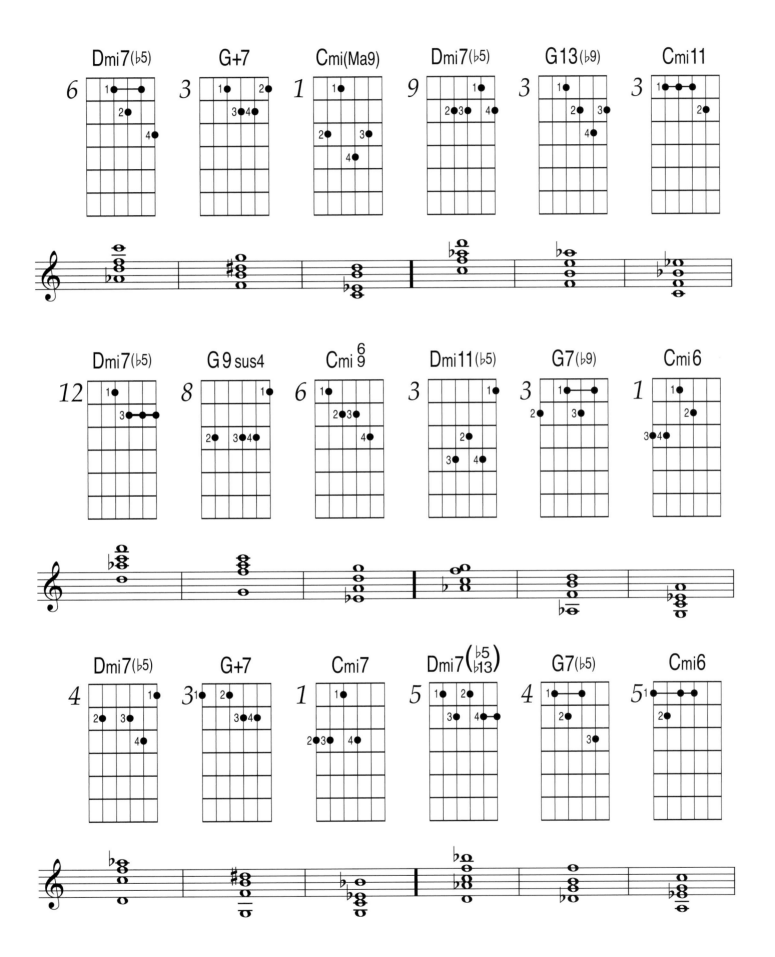

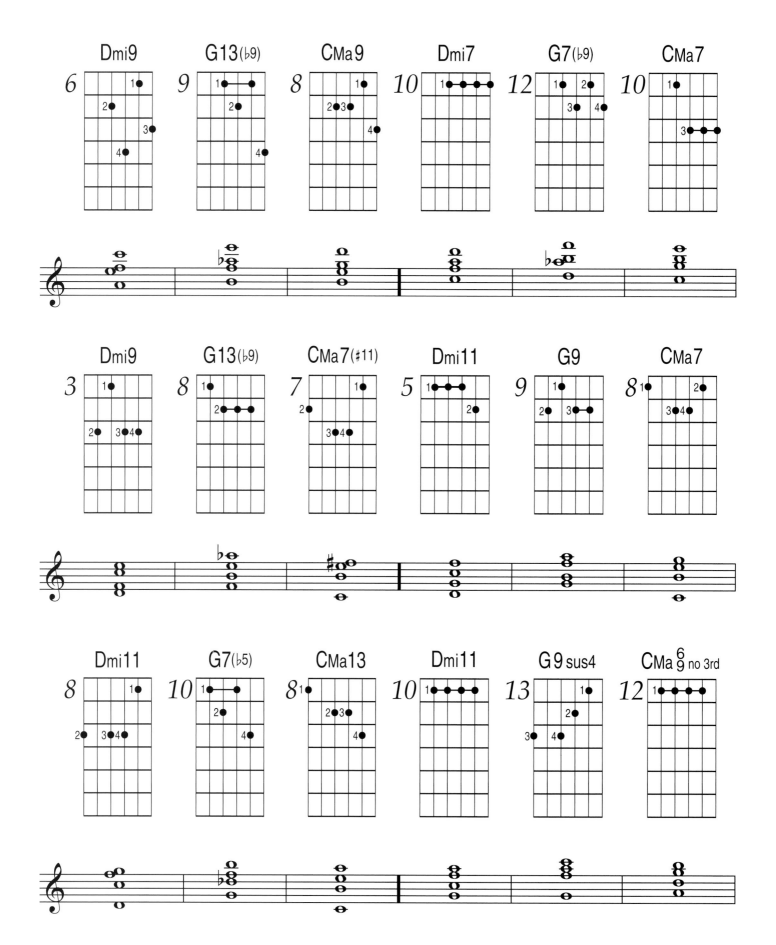

MINOR II-V-I

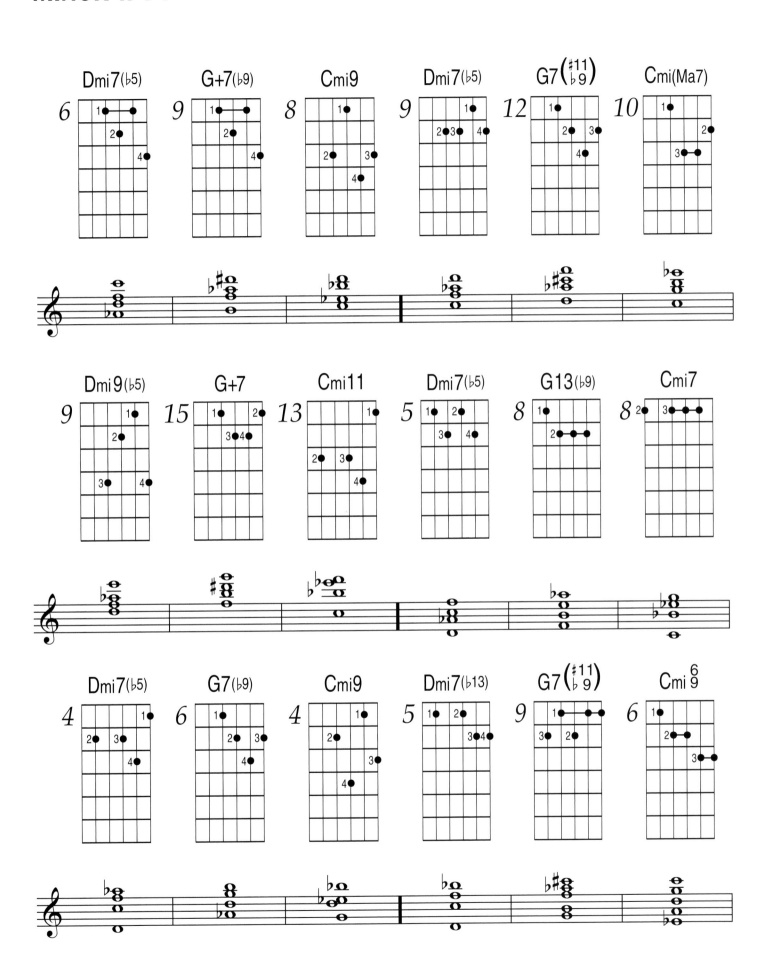

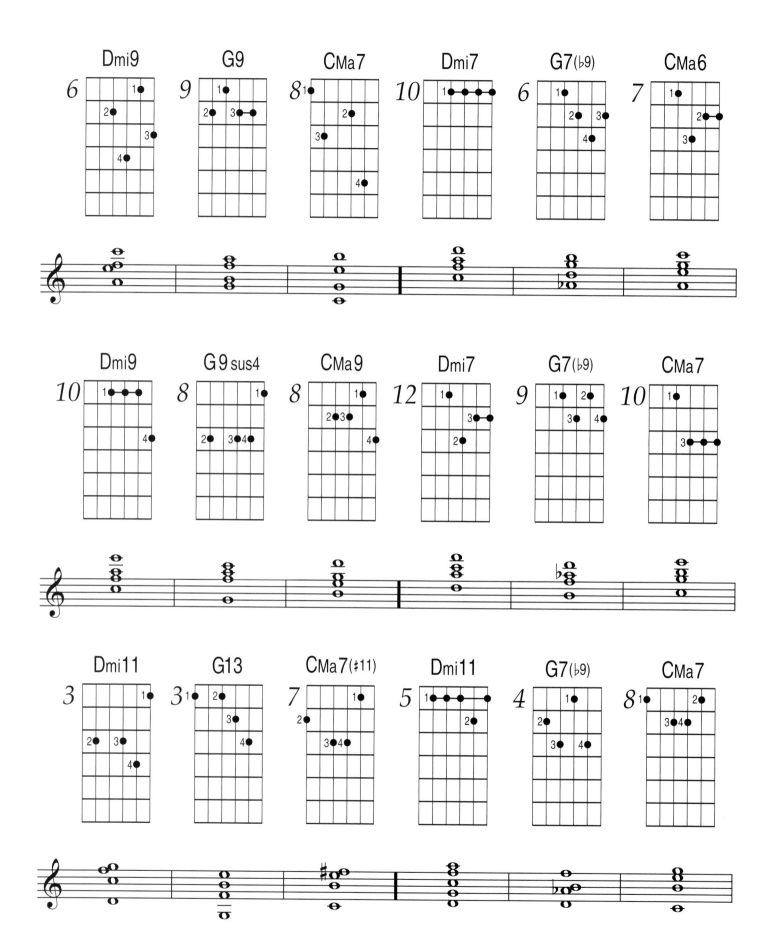

MAJOR II-V-I

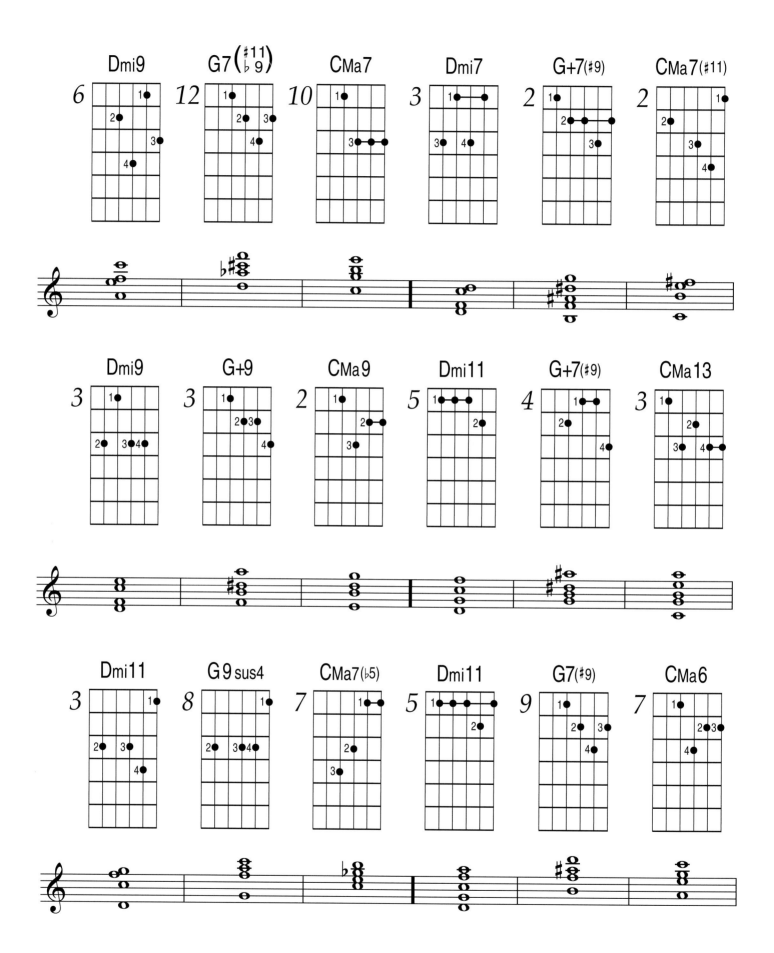

MINOR II-V-I

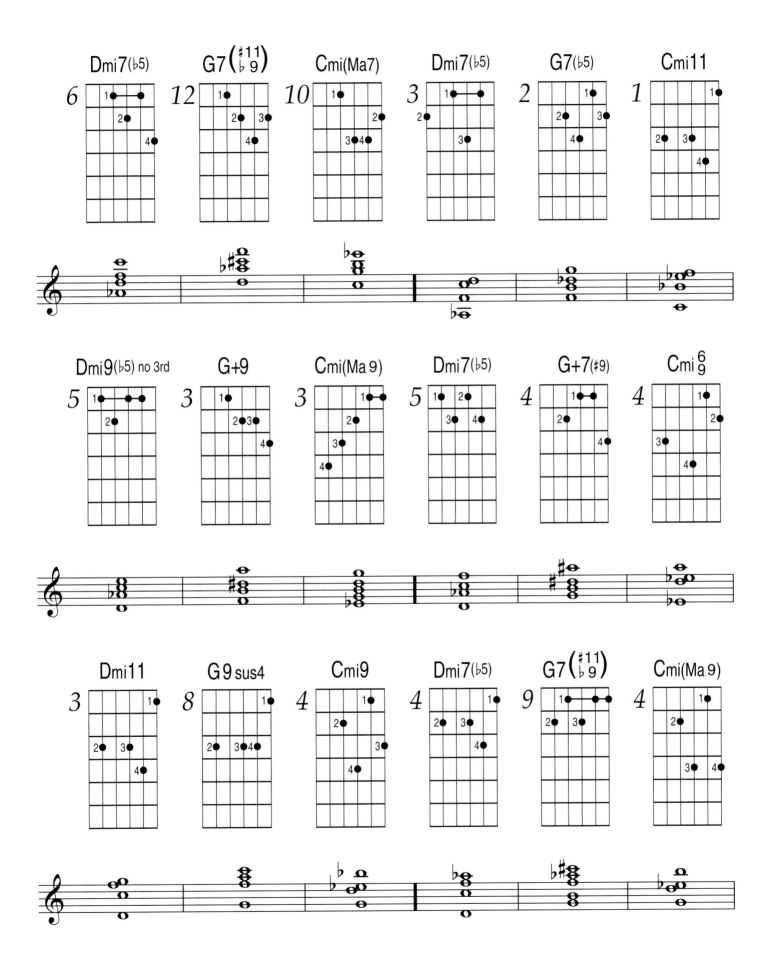

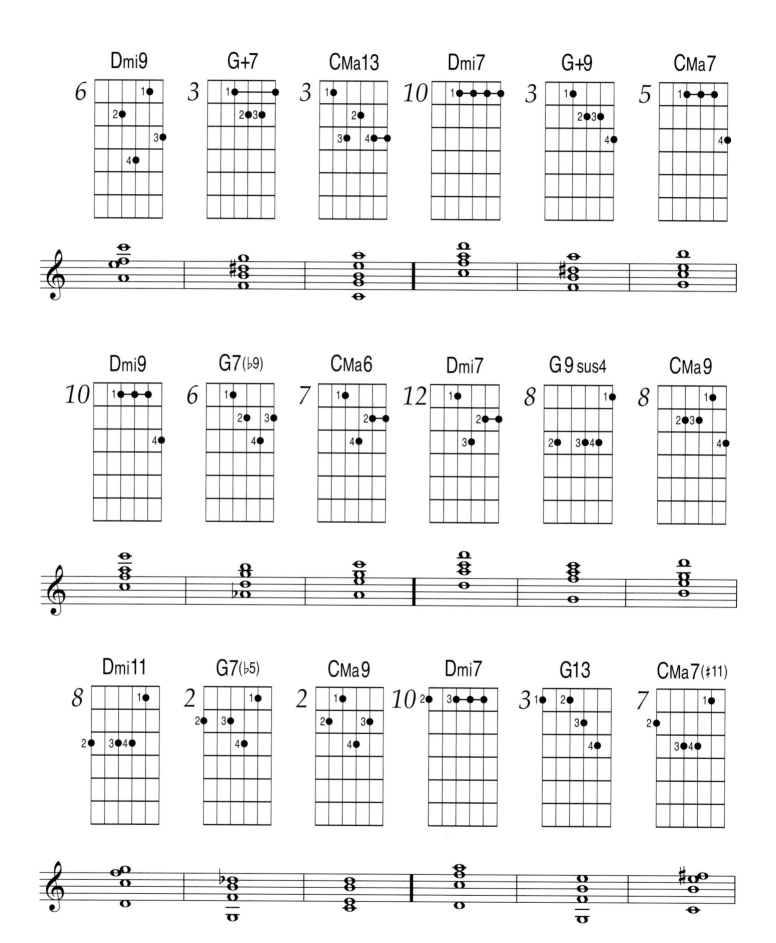

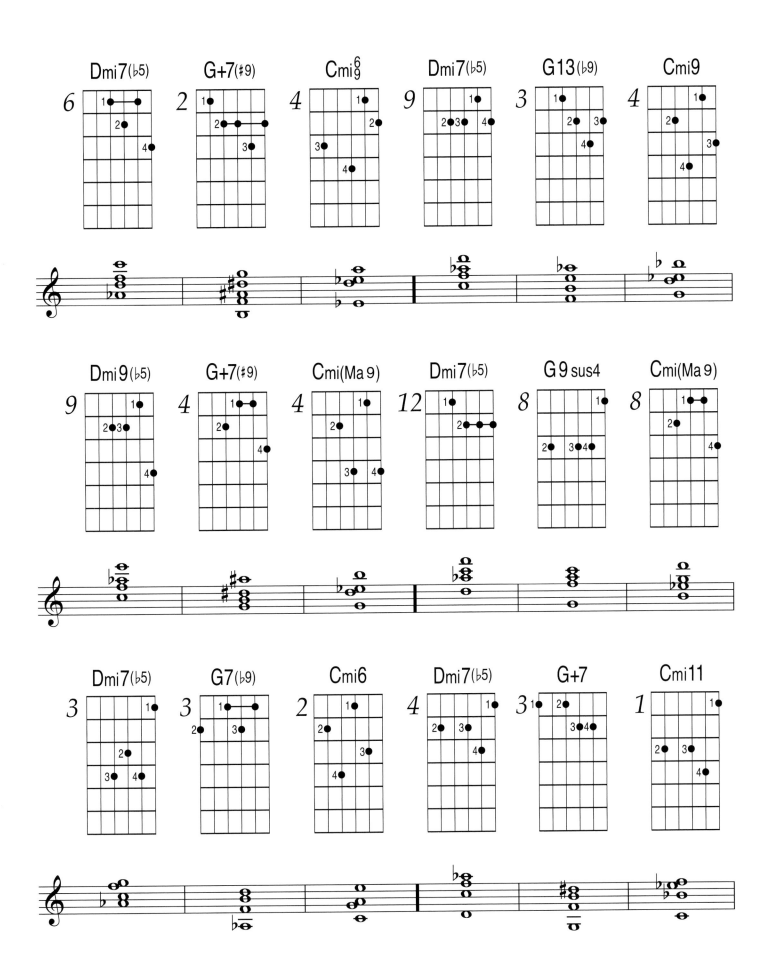

SECTION II

APPLICATION OF MELODIC CHORDS
TO MAJOR AND MINOR BLUES PROGRESSIONS

In this section, we have included excerpts from my **Major Blues for Guitar Vol. I** and **Minor Blues for Guitar Vol. I**. On pages 26-31 are examples of major and minor blues melodic chord progressions connected by either common tones or 2nds. Each chord duration is either a half or whole note. On pages 32-39 are examples of major and minor blues **melodic chord** progressions using quarter-note-duration chords. Look at the melodies created and figure out what intervals connect the chords.

MINOR BLUES

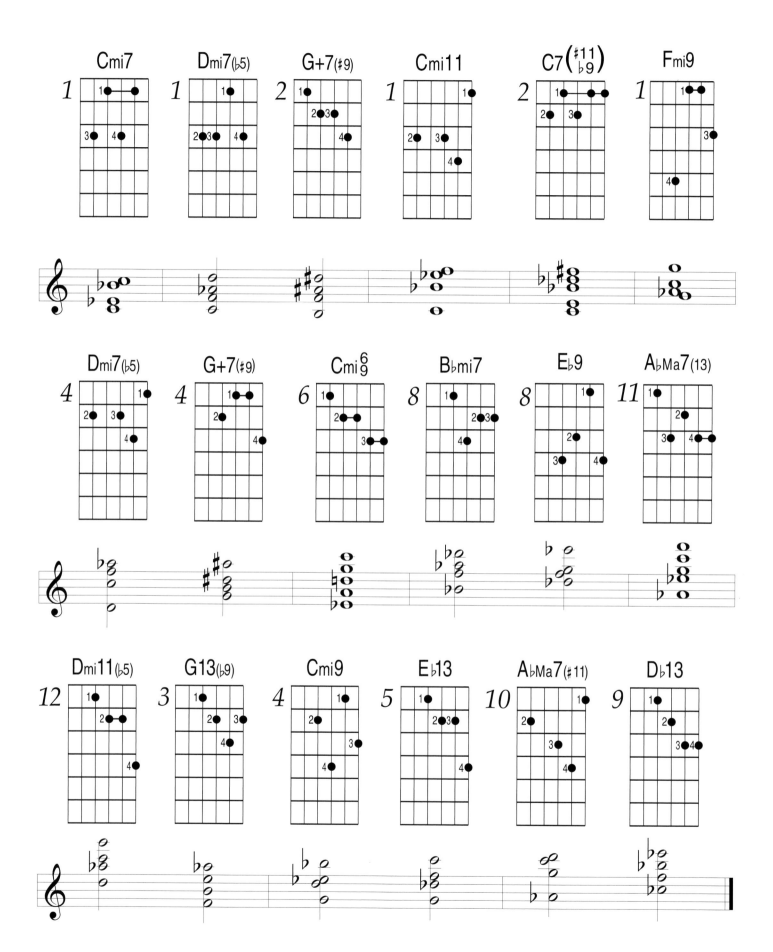

MINOR BLUES

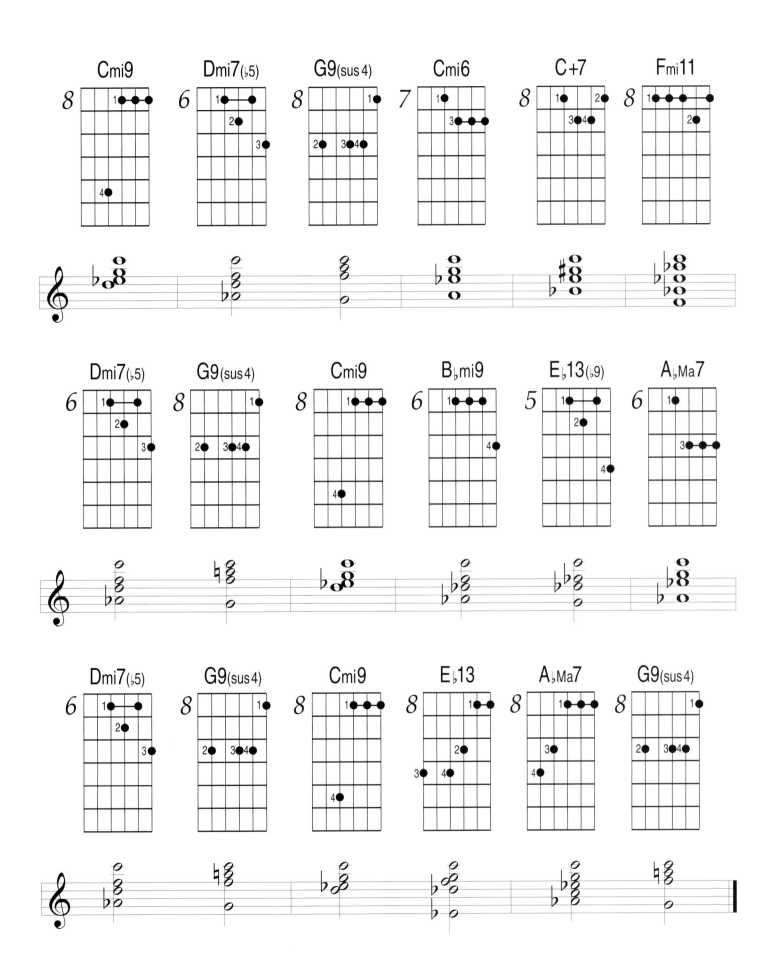

MINOR BLUES

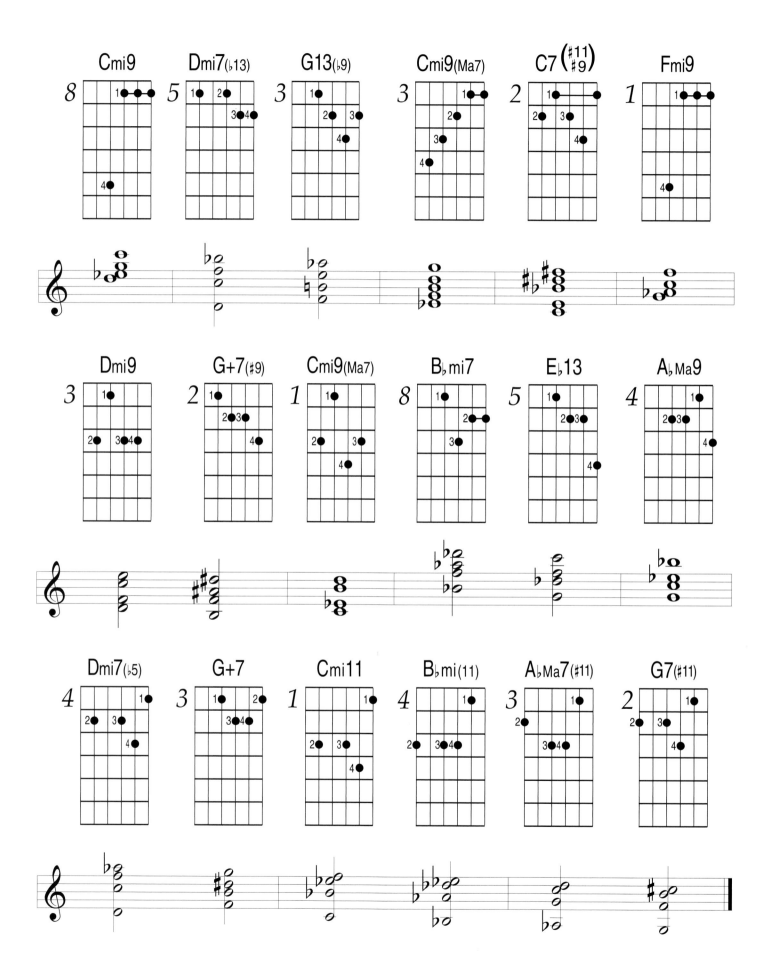

MAJOR BLUES

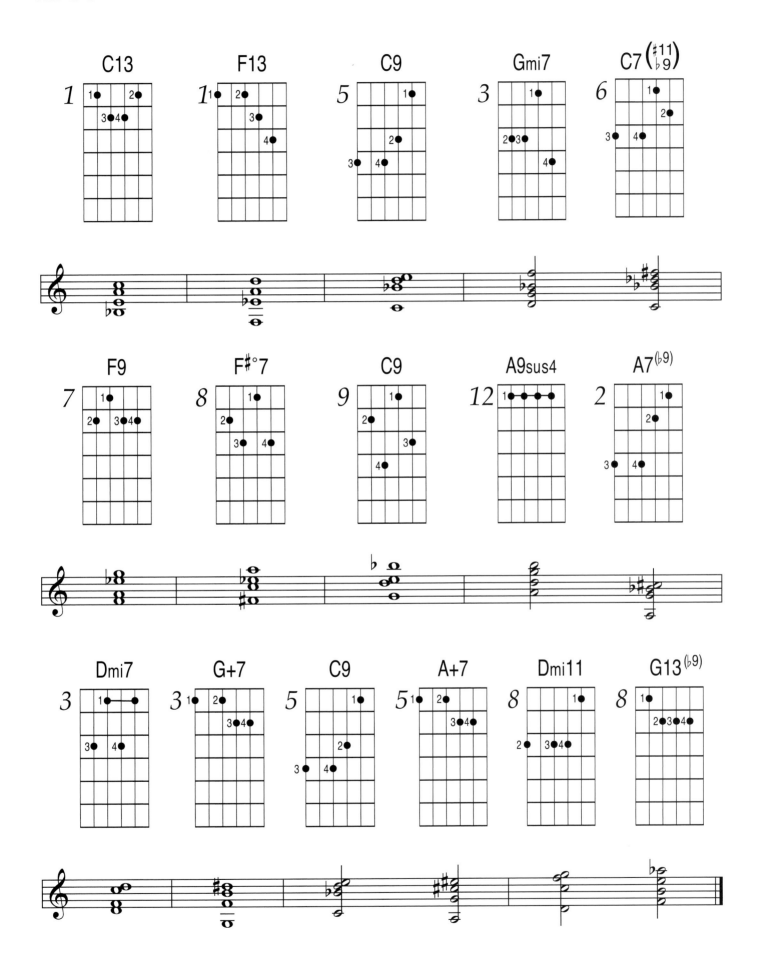

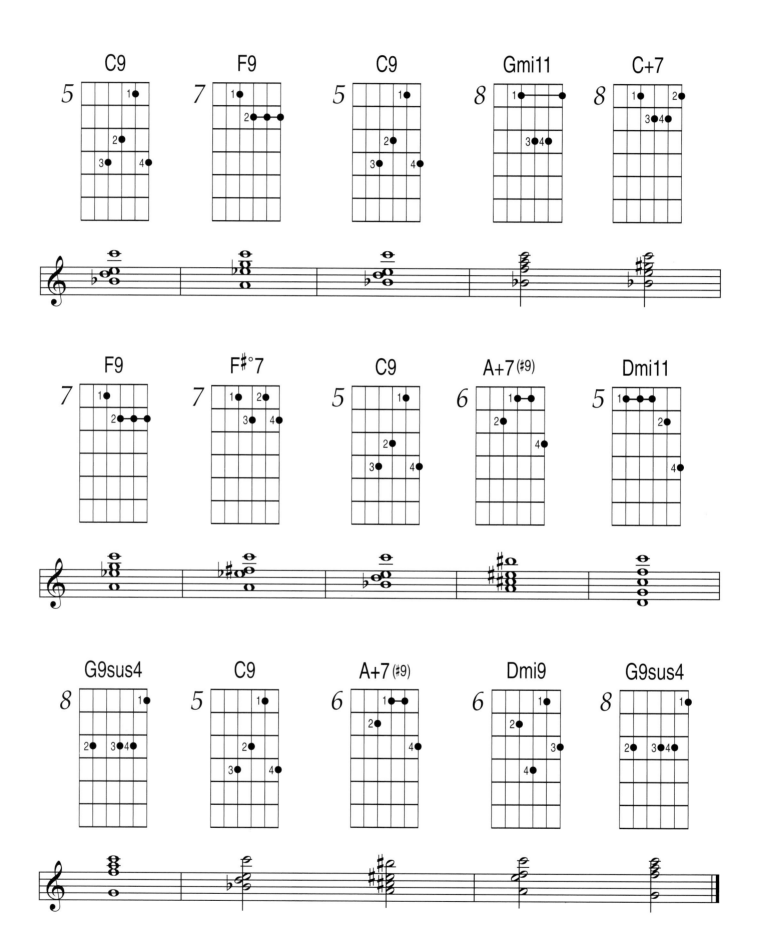

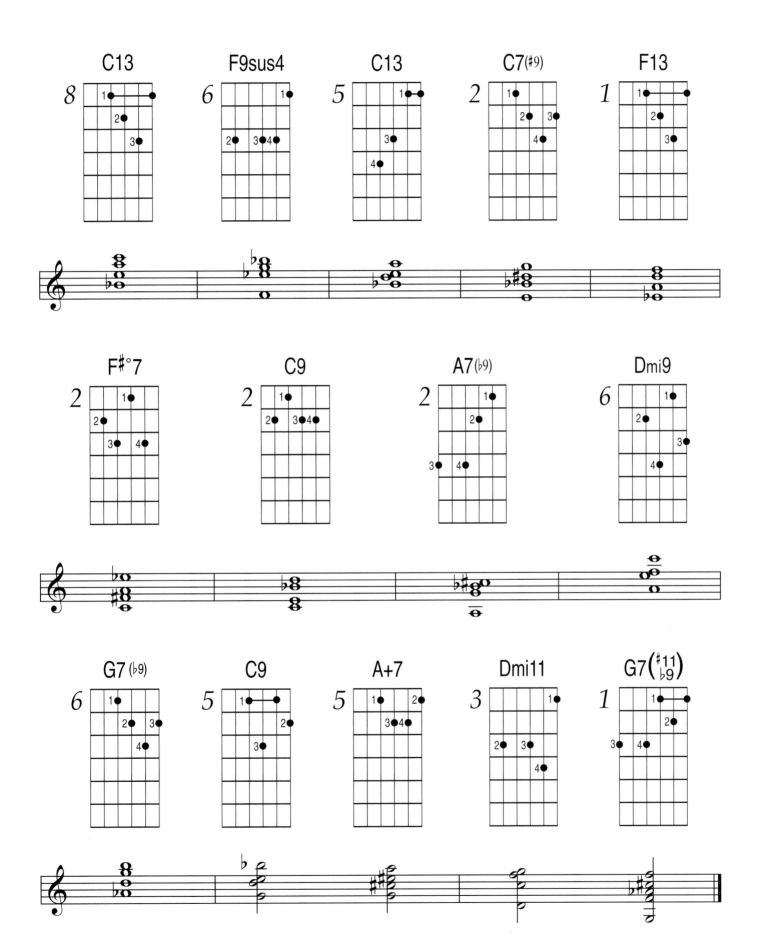

BLUES FOR JOE PASS

David Bloom

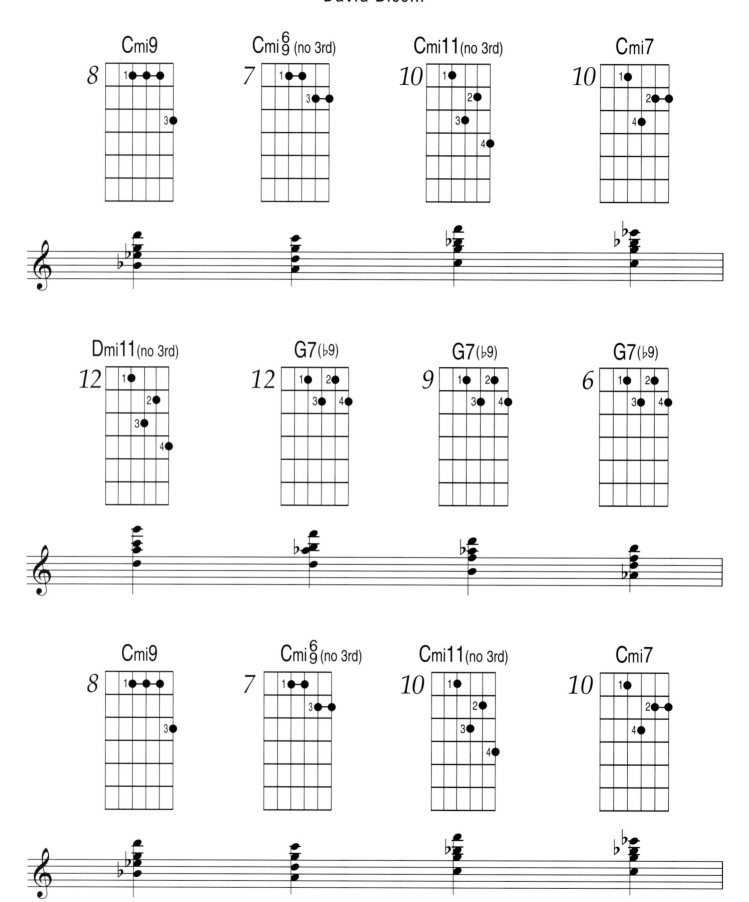

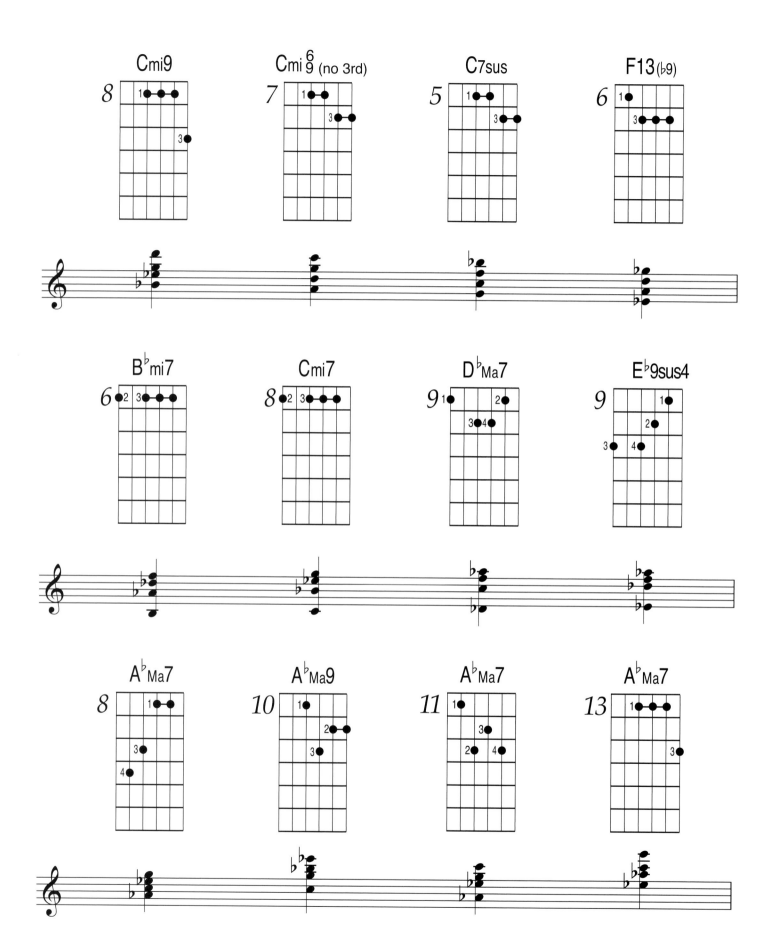

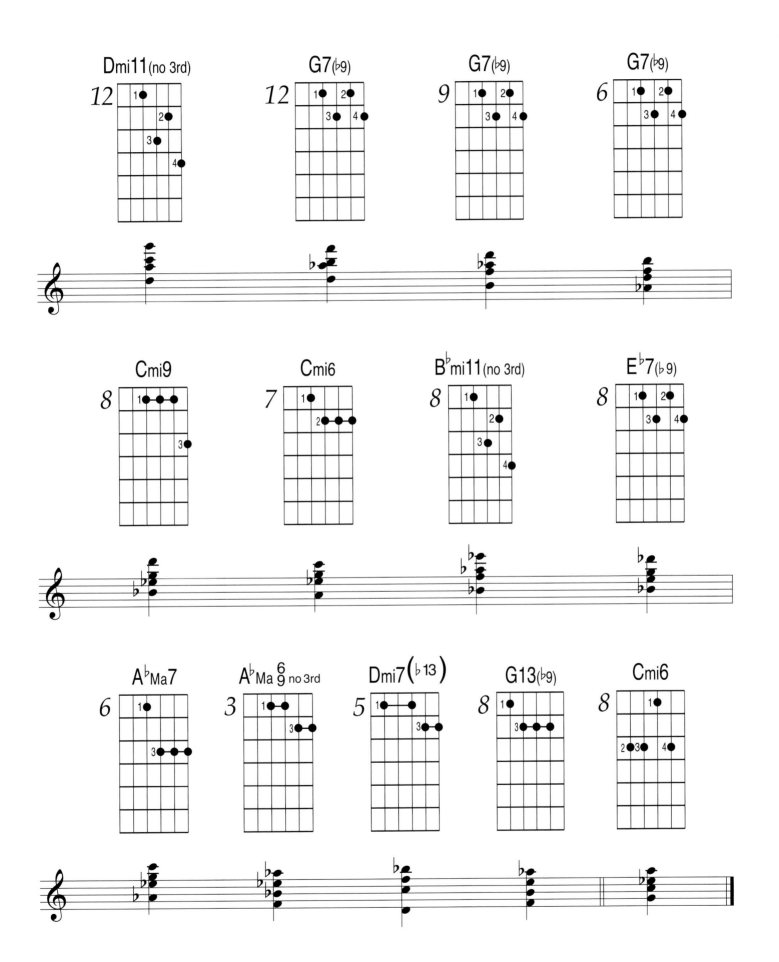

BLUES FOR FREDDY GREEN

David Bloom

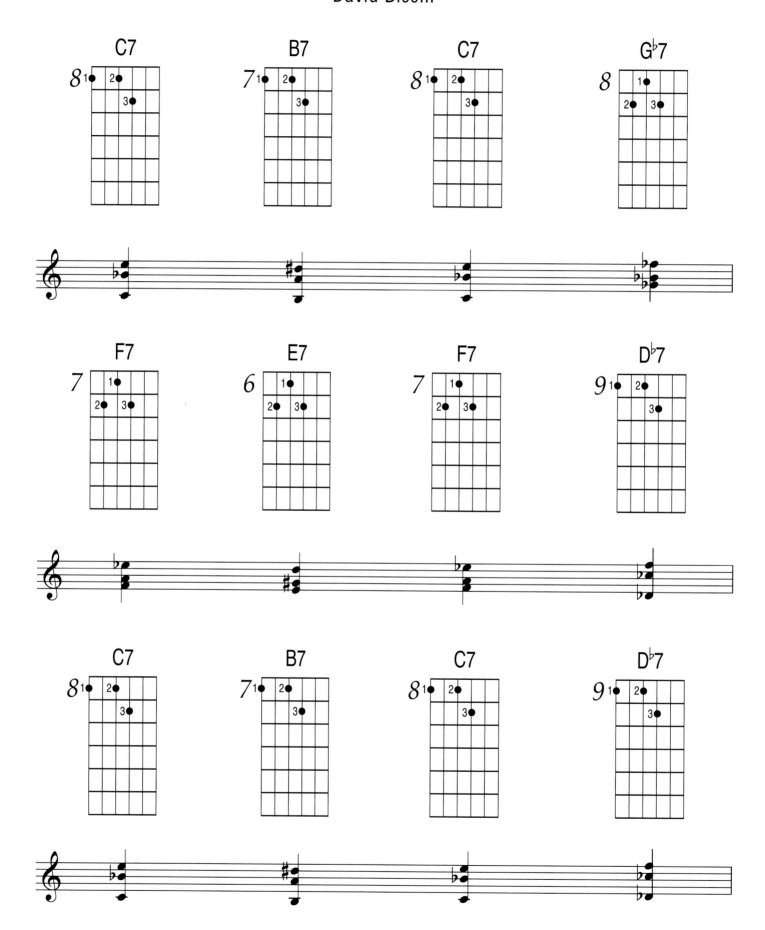

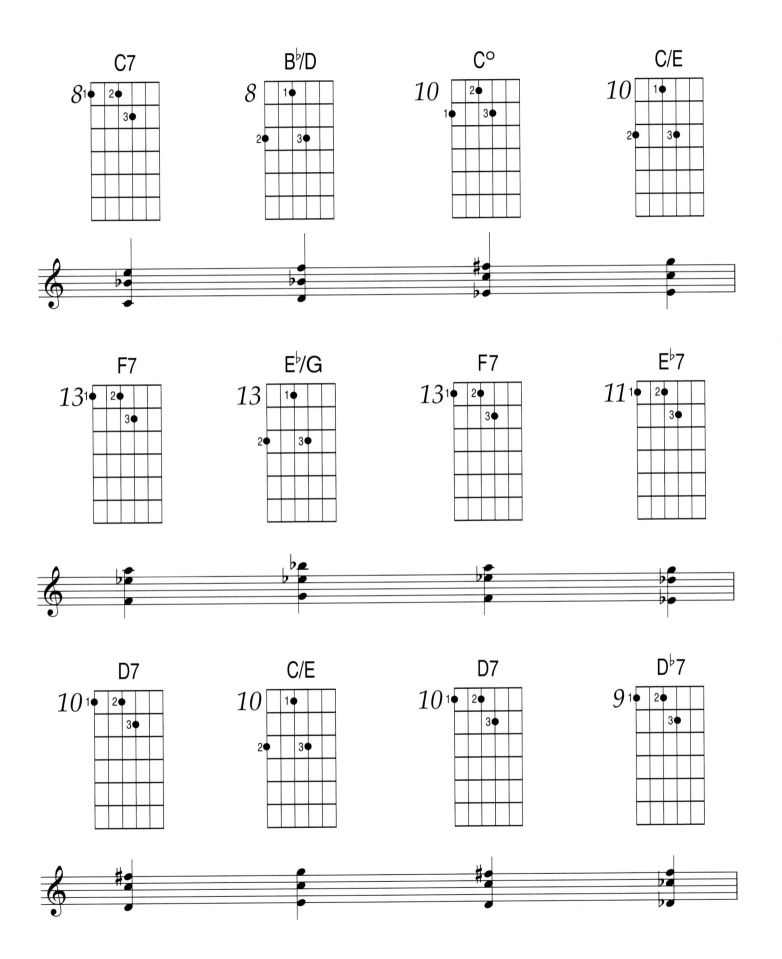

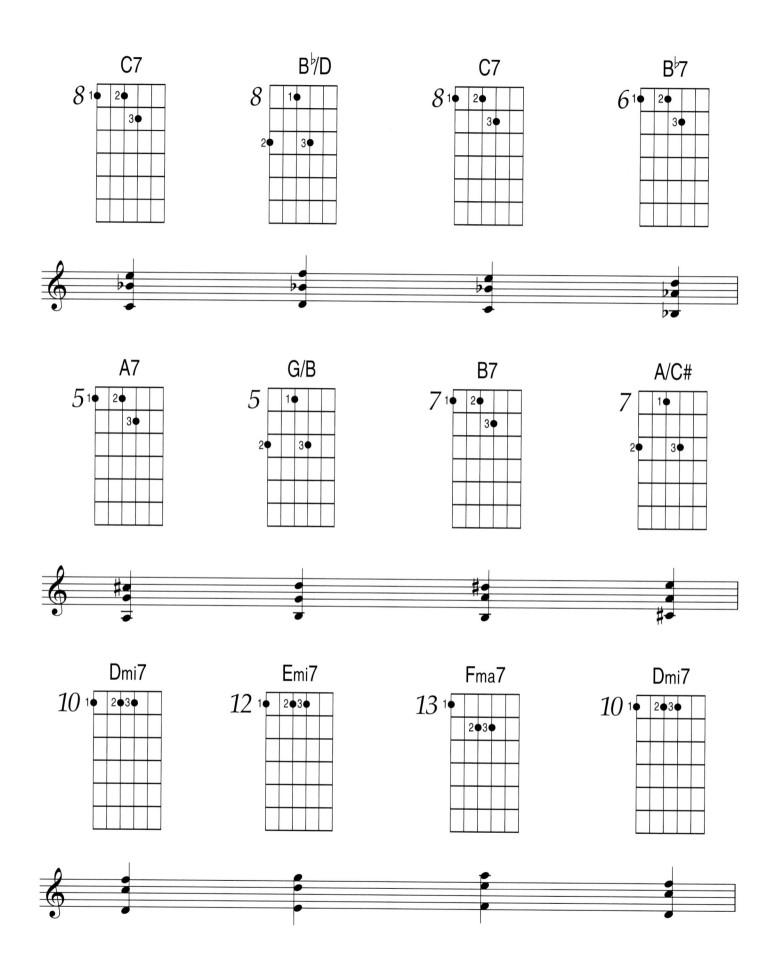

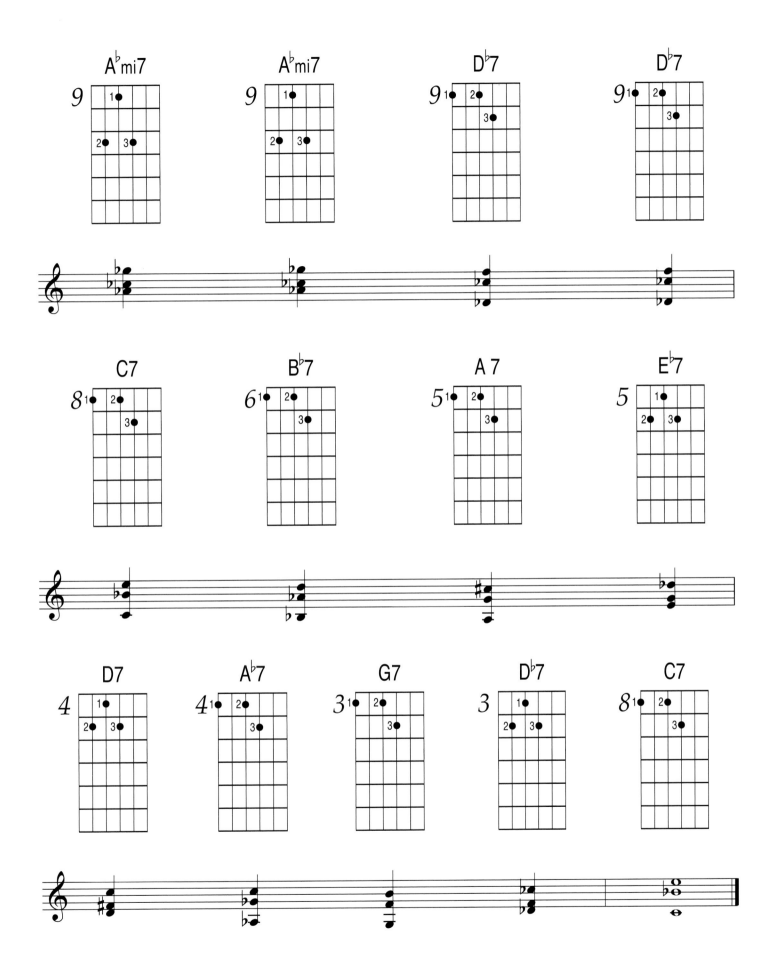

SECTION III
APPLICATION OF MELODIC CHORDS
TO CHORD-MELODY

On pages 42-46 is an arrangement of "Greensleeves." I have taken certain harmonic liberties, changing some of the original harmonies in order to create more interest - and also putting my signature on the arrangement. The melody is re-harmonized or re-colored when new chords are used with the existing melody. Anyone who knows the tune will recognize the melody but will also hear different chords. Chord-melody song arrangements are a great vehicle to personalize standard songs and show the listener your point of view, which is critical in great music.

GREENSLEEVES

Arranged by David Bloom

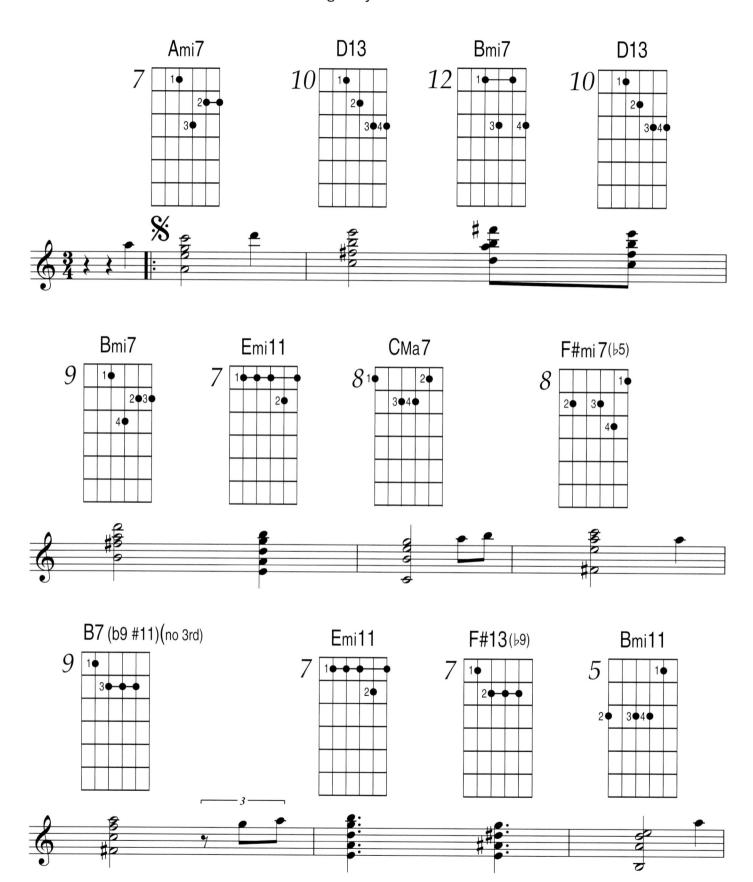

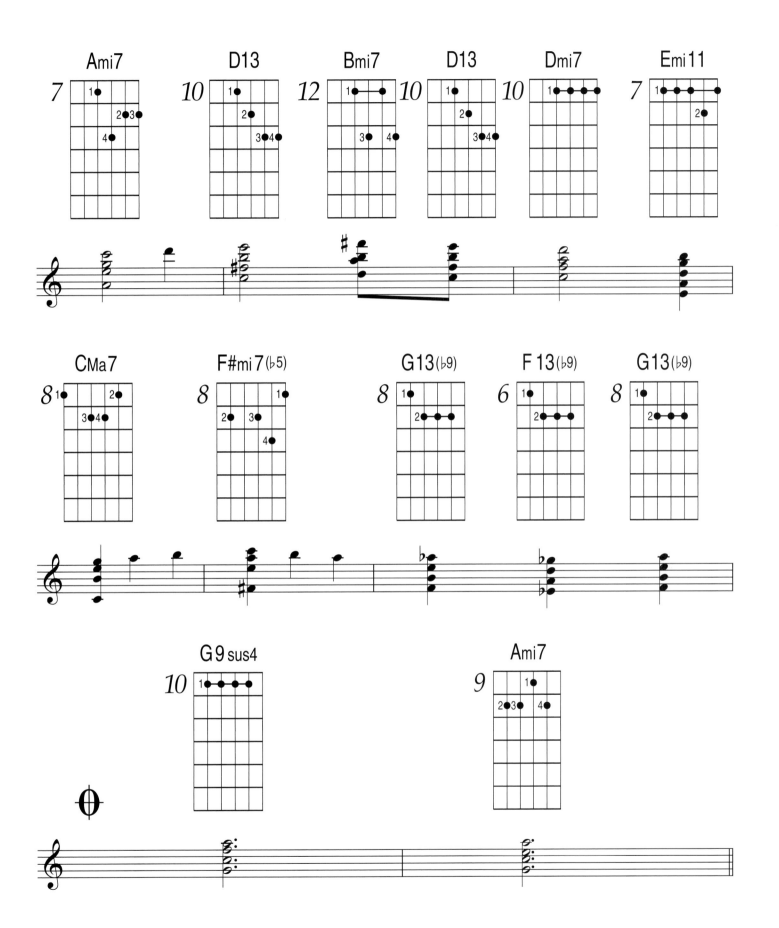

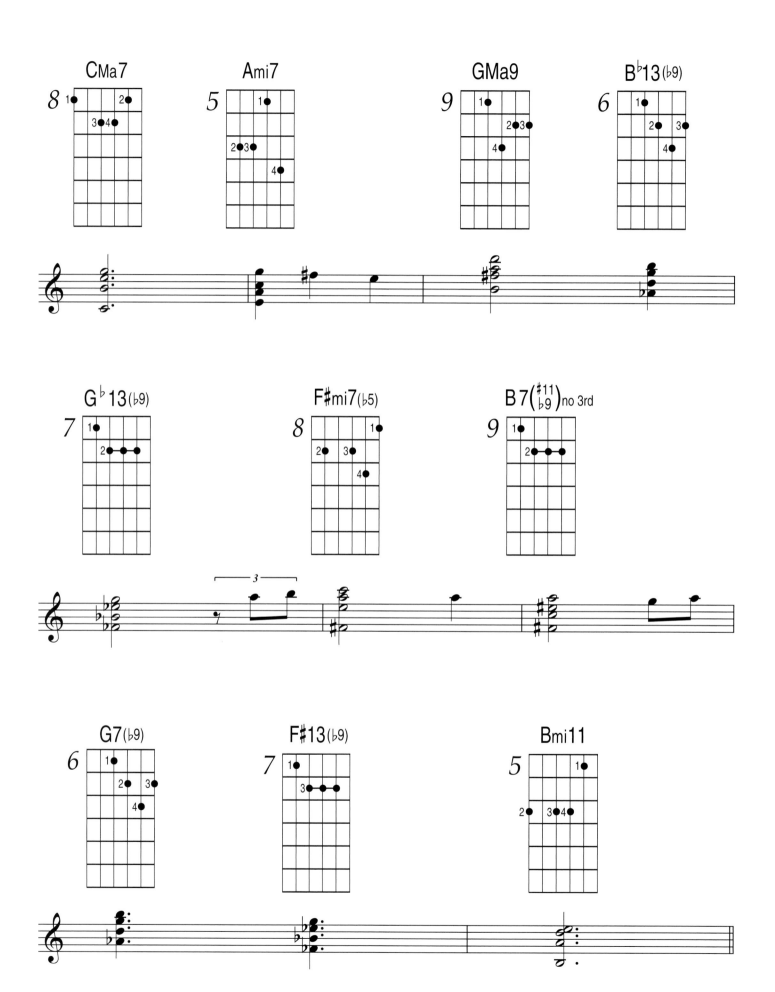

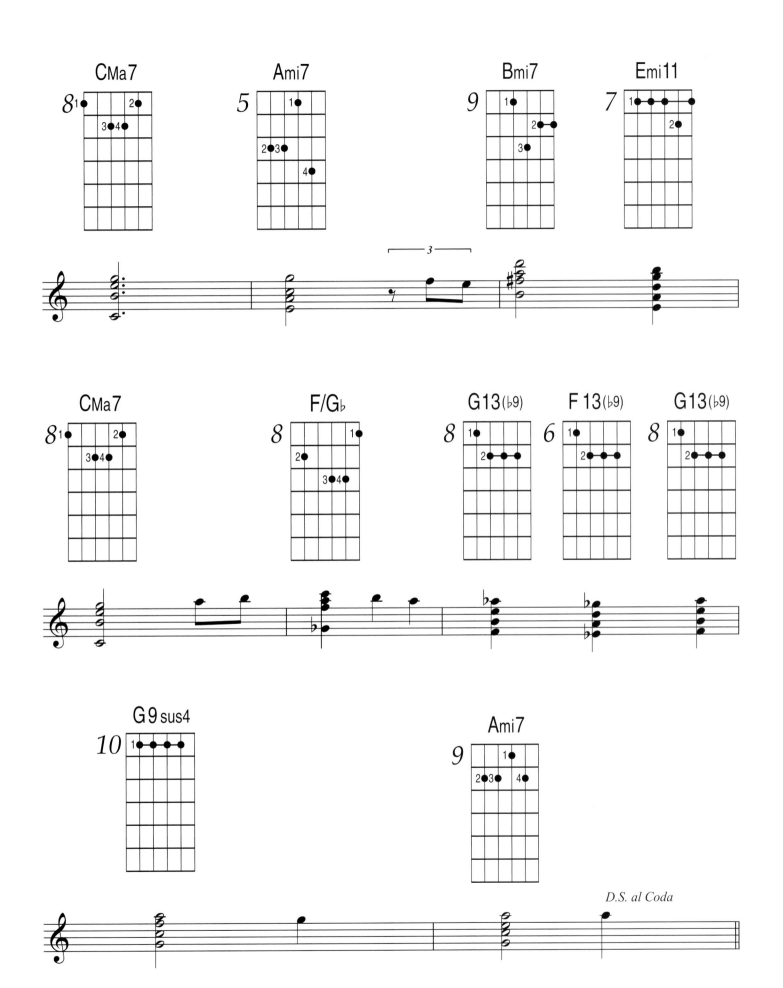

D.S. al Coda

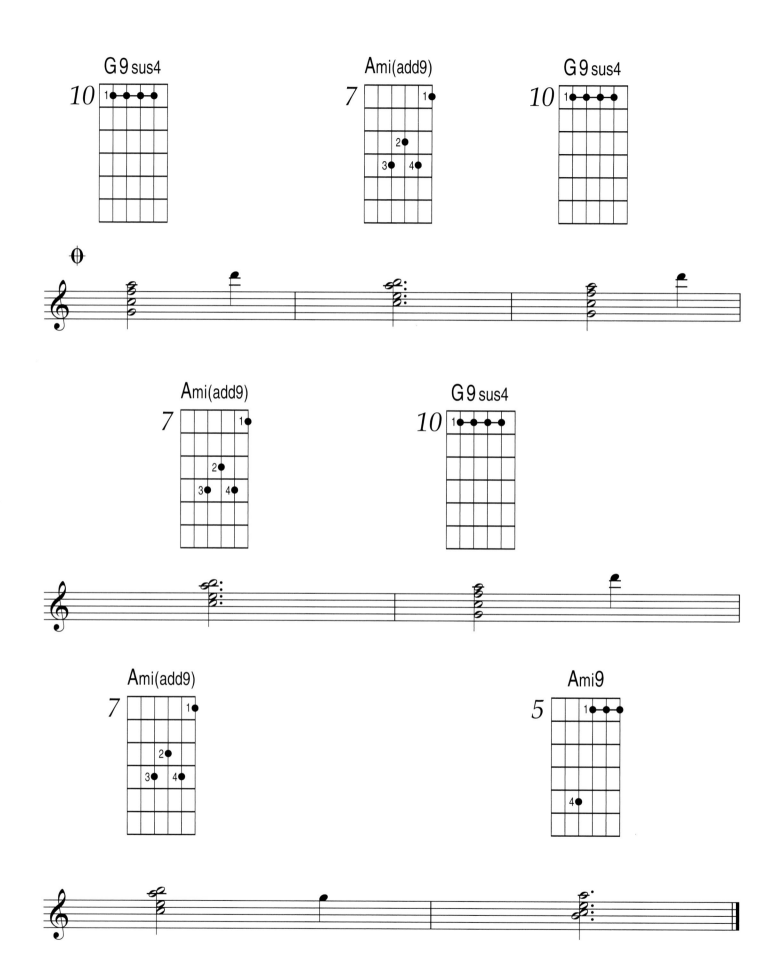

SECTION IV

APPLICATION OF MELODIC CHORDS
TO COMPING ON STANDARD PROGRESSIONS

In this section Peter Lerner, one of my professional students, has provided comping (for accompaniment) chords to a very common jazz progression (you figure out which one). On pages 48-50, the melody ascends by seconds throughout the progression and only changes direction if it drops down an octave due to the range of the guitar. Similarly, from pages 51-53, the melody descends by seconds and only changes direction due to the range of the guitar.

MELODIC COMPING CHORDS FOR STANDARD PROGRESSIONS

by Peter Lerner

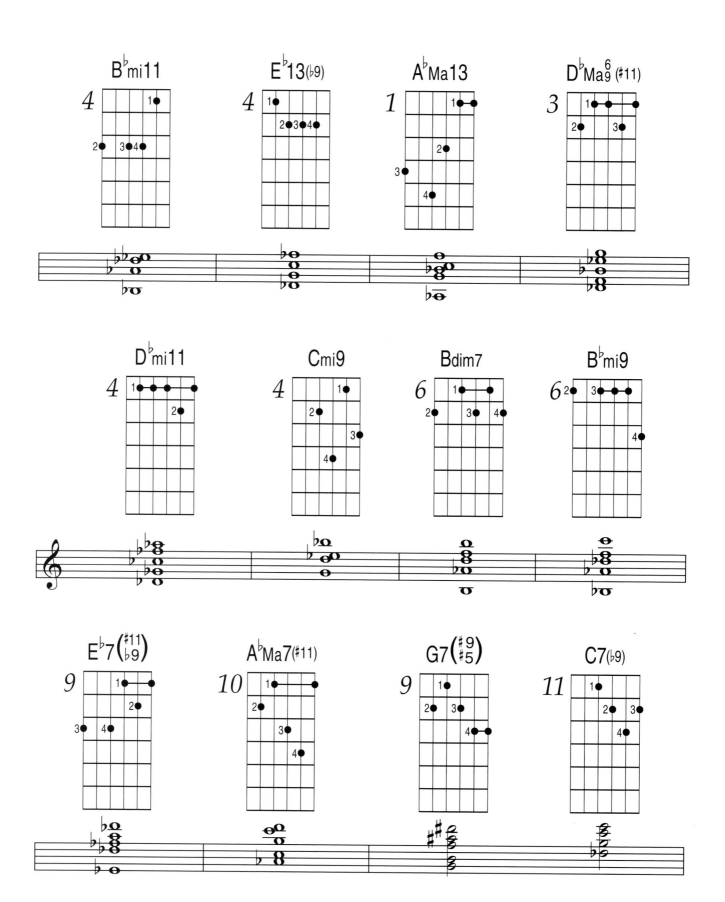

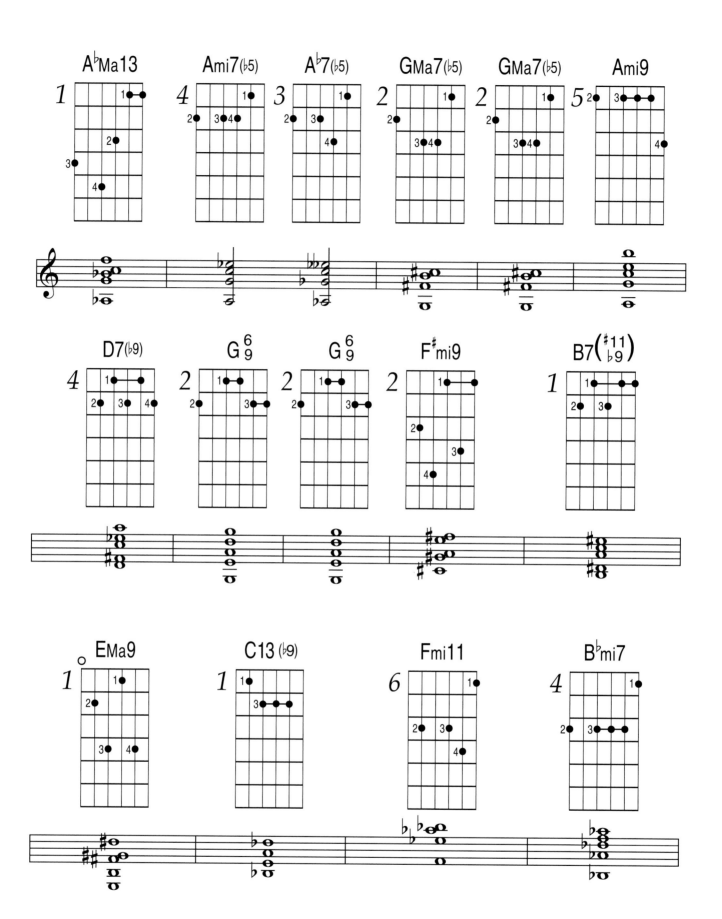

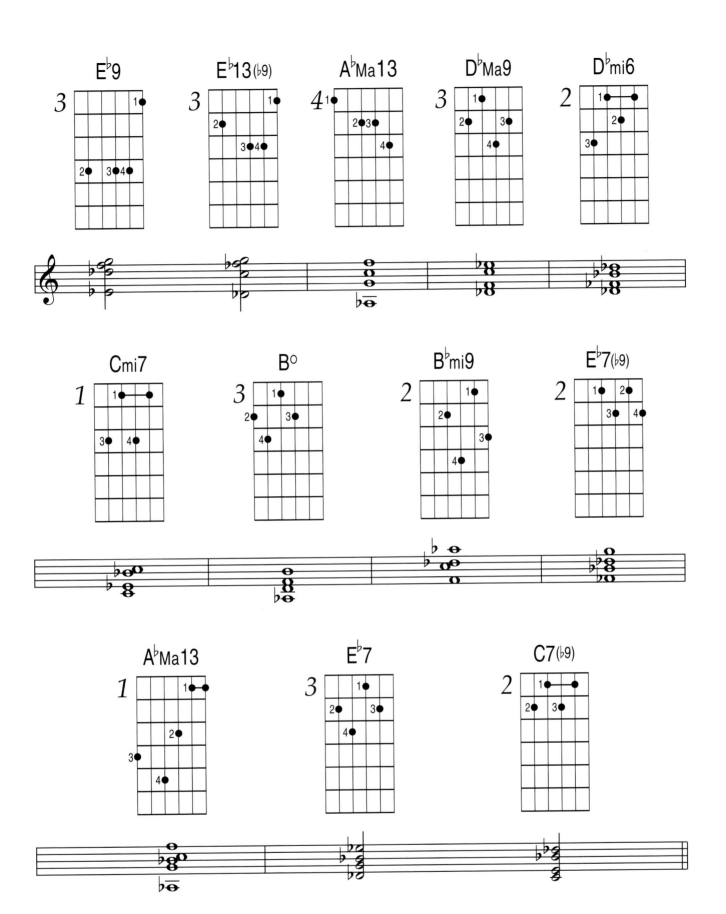

SECTION V

APPLICATION OF MELODIC CHORDS
TO CHORD SOLOING

Lee Metcalf, another of my professional students, has contributed an interesting chord solo on another popular jazz standard. A chord solo means that instead of improvising with single-note melodies, chords are used. This solo uses chords and not just melodies. Chord soloing technique requires fluency with the chords in this book because you have to know them instantaneously in order to improvise interesting melodies.

CHORD SOLO FOR GUITAR

by Lee Metcalf

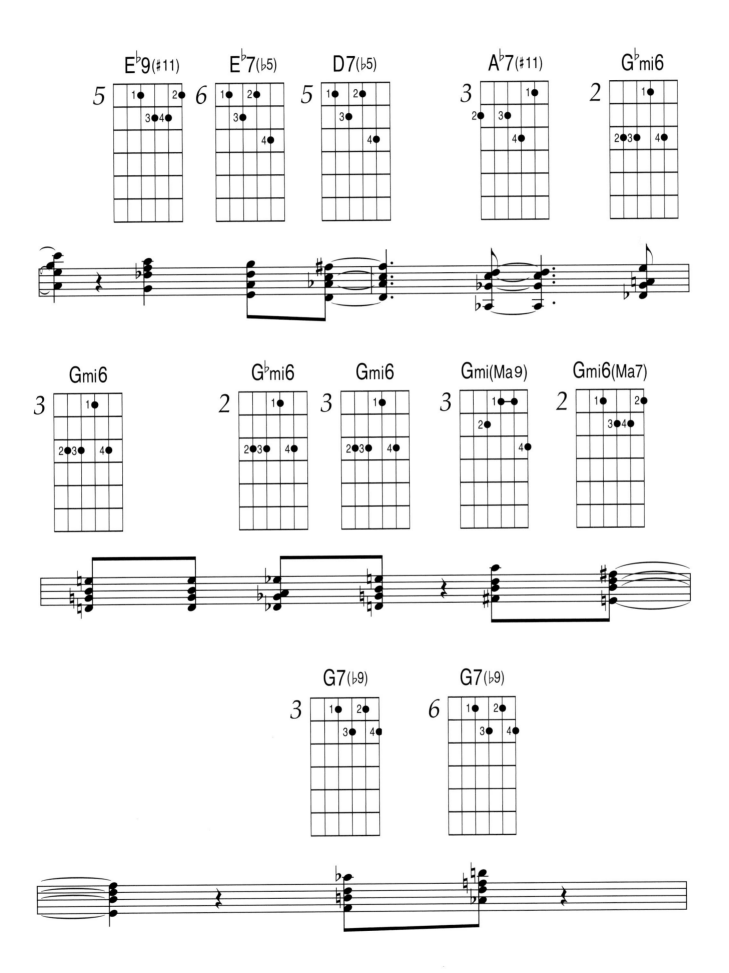

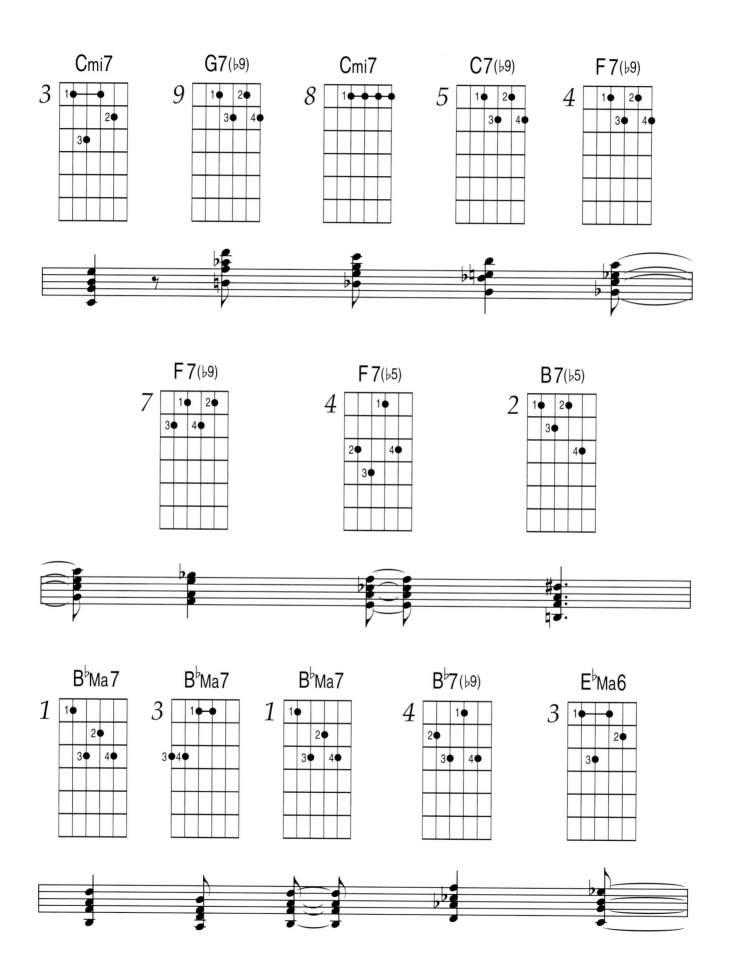

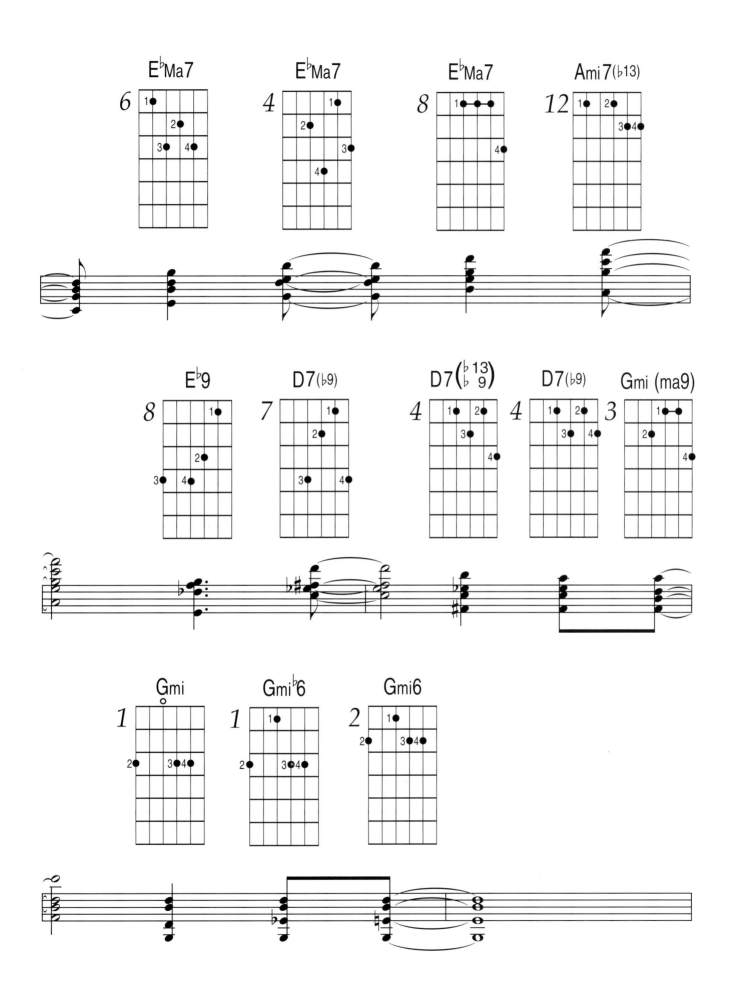

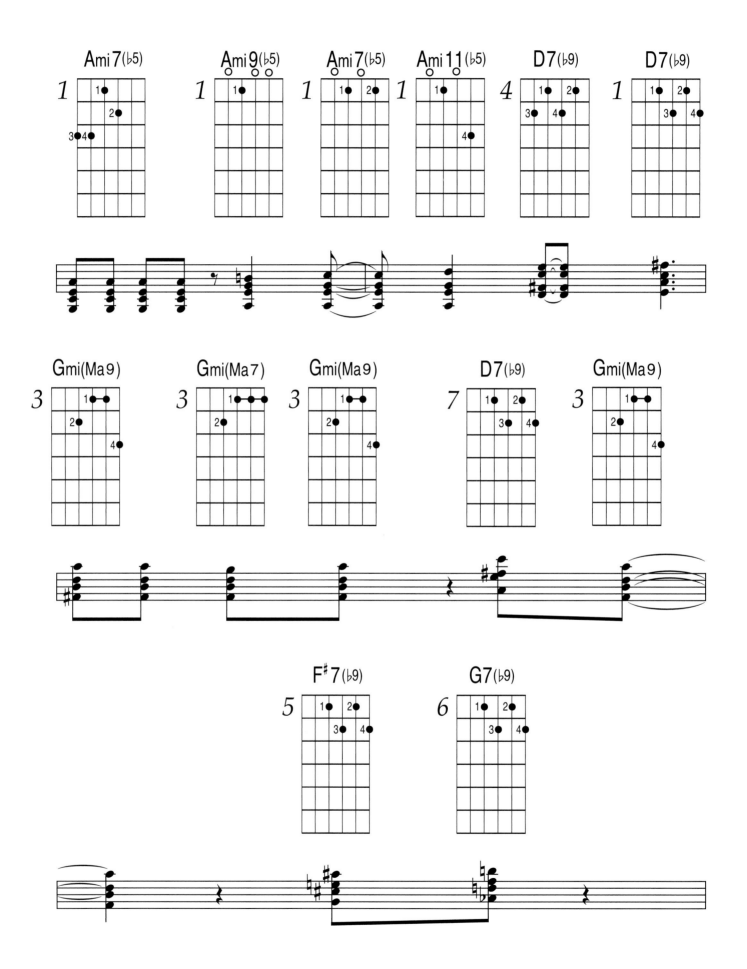

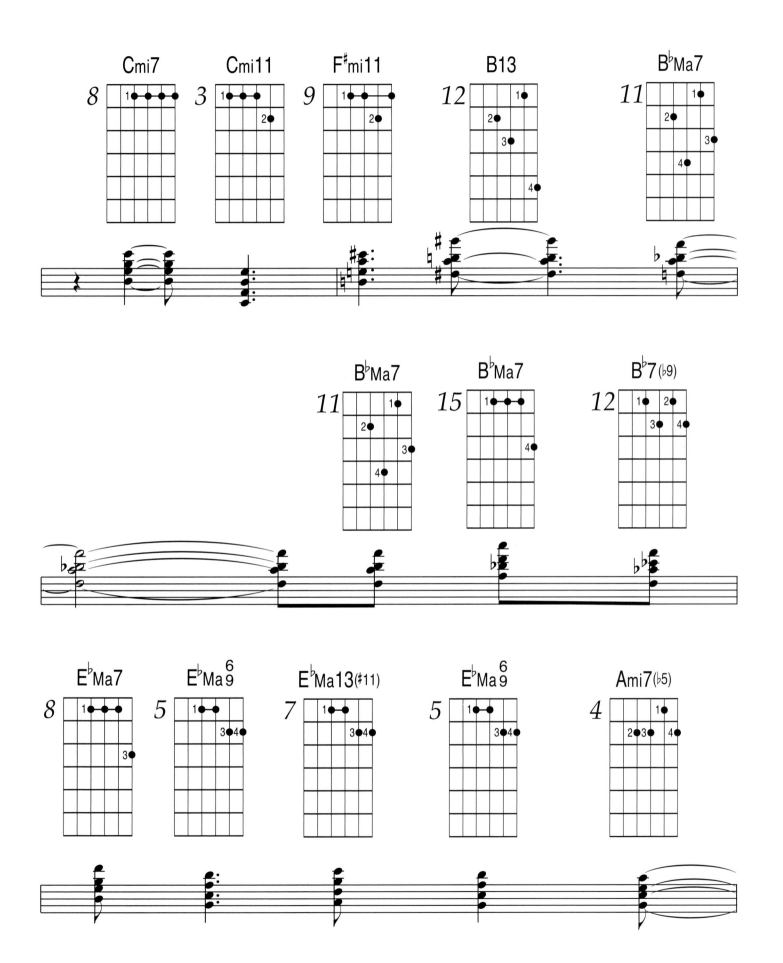

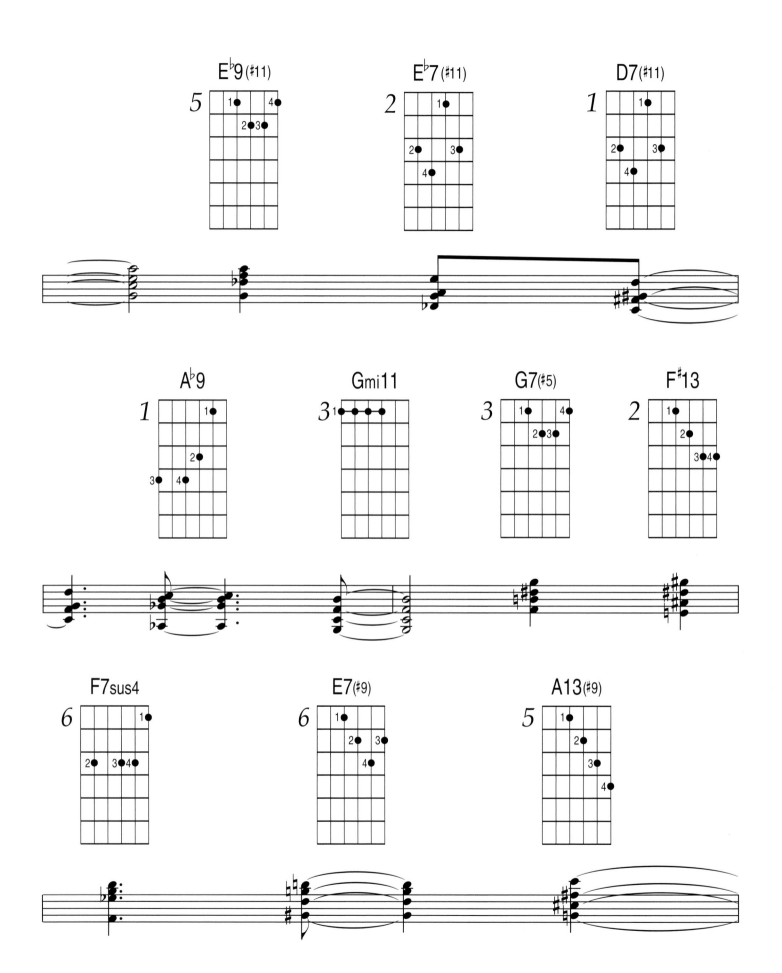

SECTION VI
MELODIC CHORD DICTIONARY

In this section I have enclosed a **melodic chord** dictionary of all the main chord types and each chord's available chord tones (notes that fit). These include the root, 3rd, 5th, 7th, and the extensions, which are the 9th, 11th, and 13th. In the major family, the root, 9th, 3rd, #4th, 5th, 6th, and 7th are the available chord tones and extensions. For example, the first page of the major family shows the root in the top right-hand corner of the page. This indicates that every chord on the page has the root in the melody (the top note of the chord). Every page in this **melodic chord** dictionary section will label both the chord family and the chord tone that's in the melody for each chord on the page. All chords in this section are based in the note C root. You can move (transpose) them to whatever key you want.

Major family

Minor family

Dominant family

Minor seventh flat five

Suspended fourth

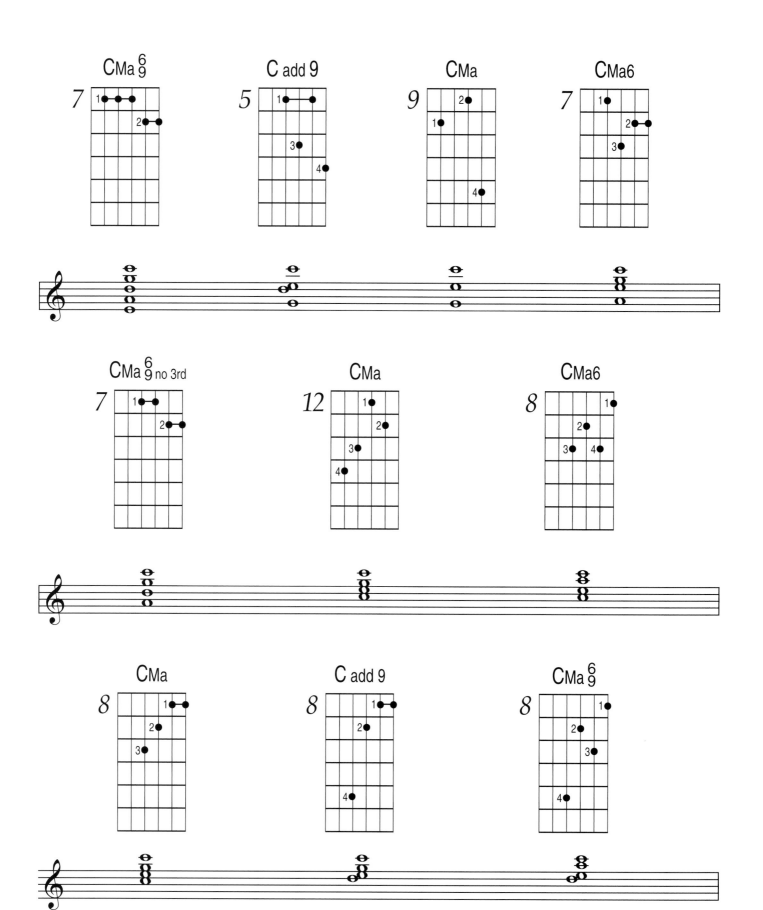

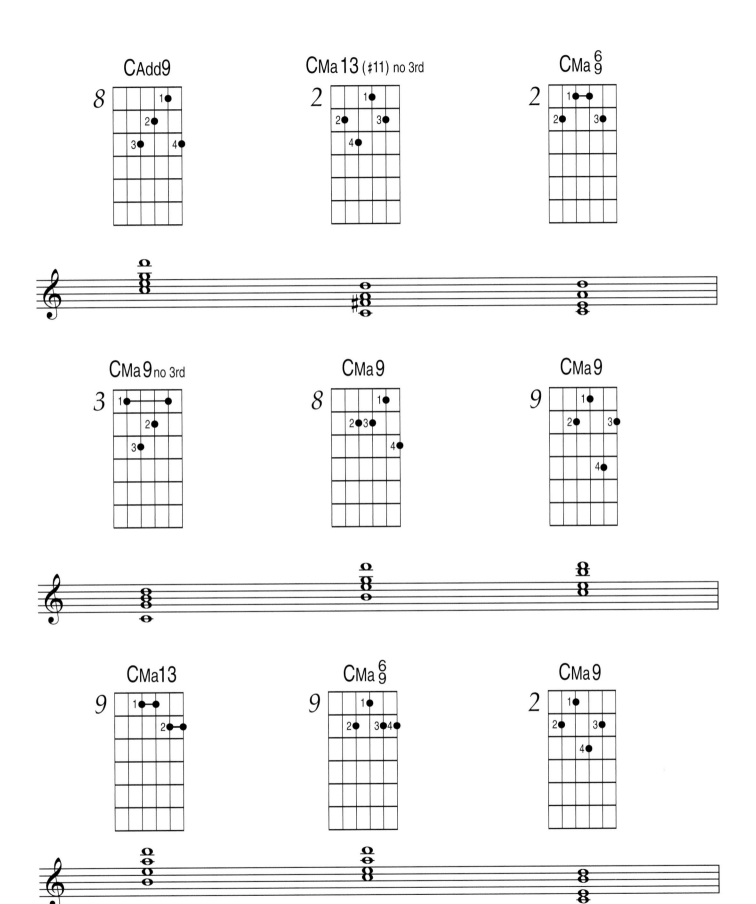

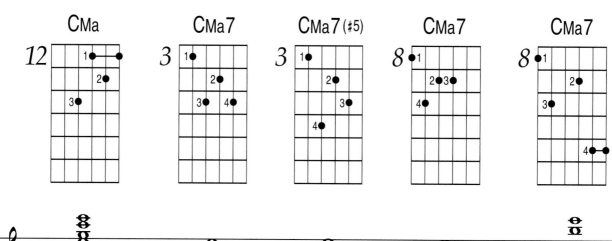

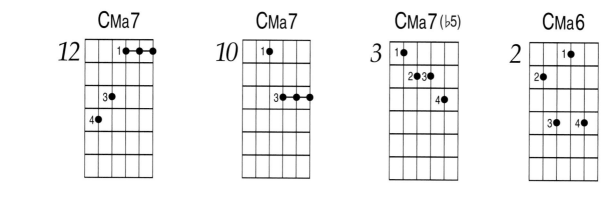

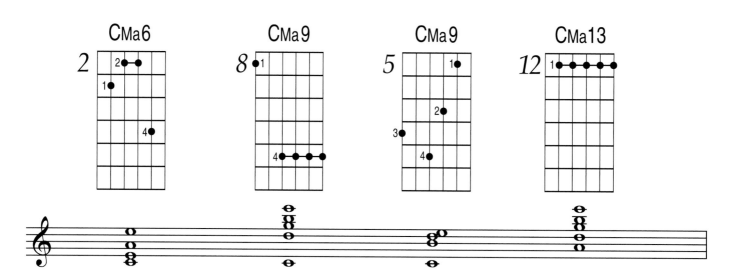

CMa7(#11)

CMa7(#11)

CMa 6/9(#11)

CMa7(#11)no 3rd

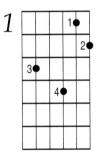

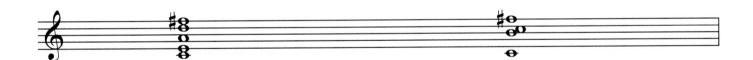

CMa7(#11)

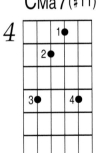

CMa9(#11)

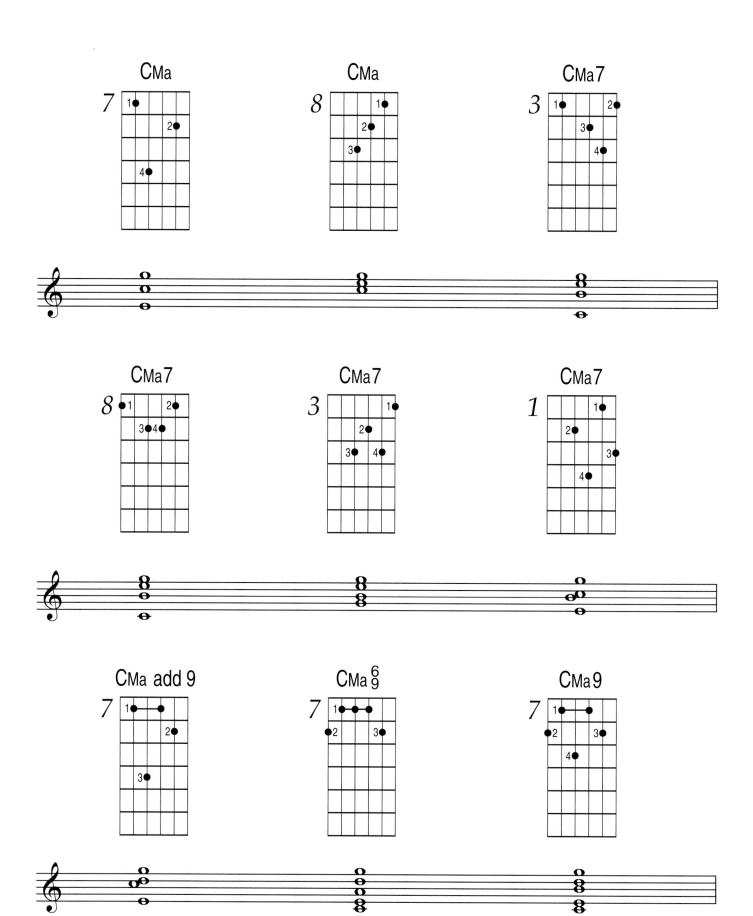

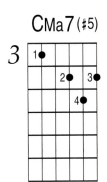

CMa7 (#5)

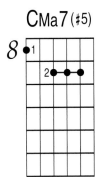

CMa7 (#5)

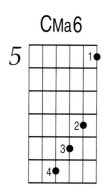

CMa6

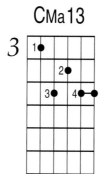

CMa13

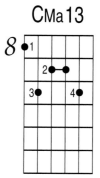

CMa13

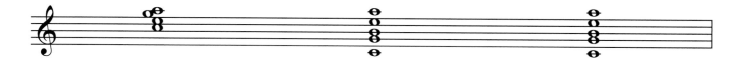

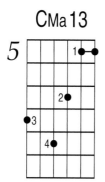

CMa13

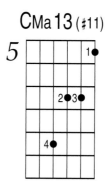

CMa13 (#11)

CMa6

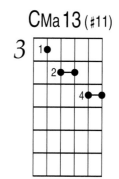

CMa13 (#11)

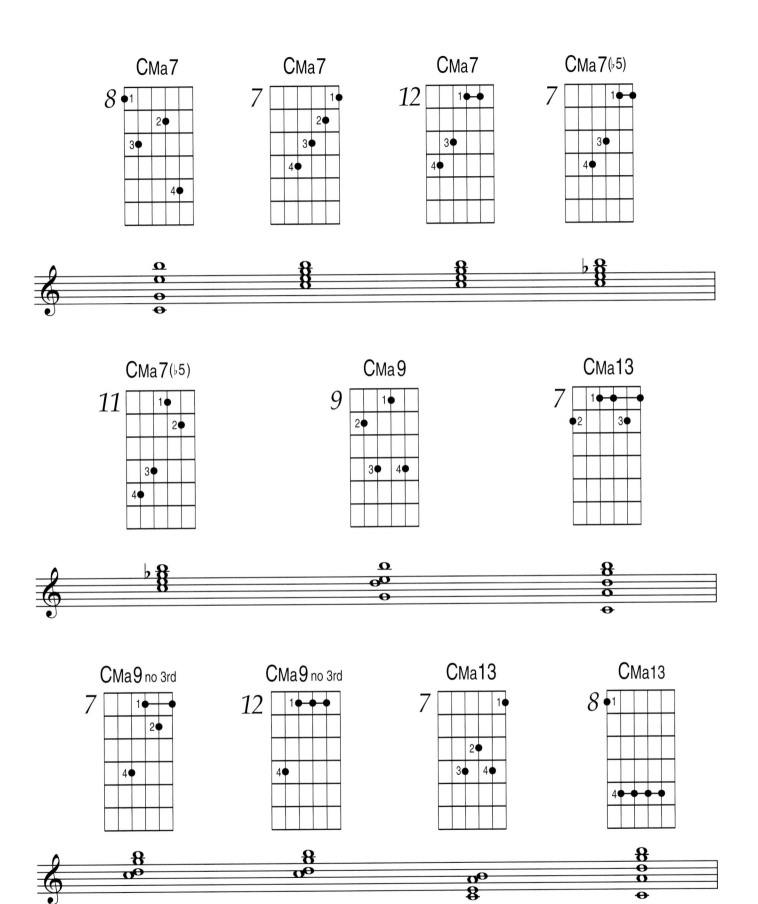

MINOR

Root

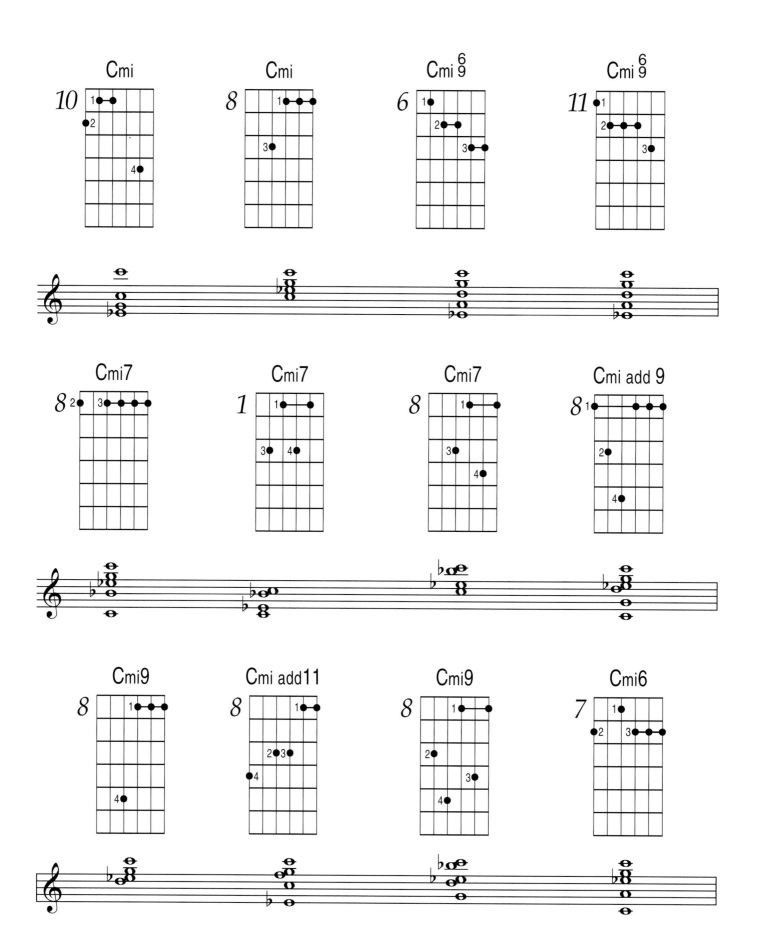

-74-

MINOR

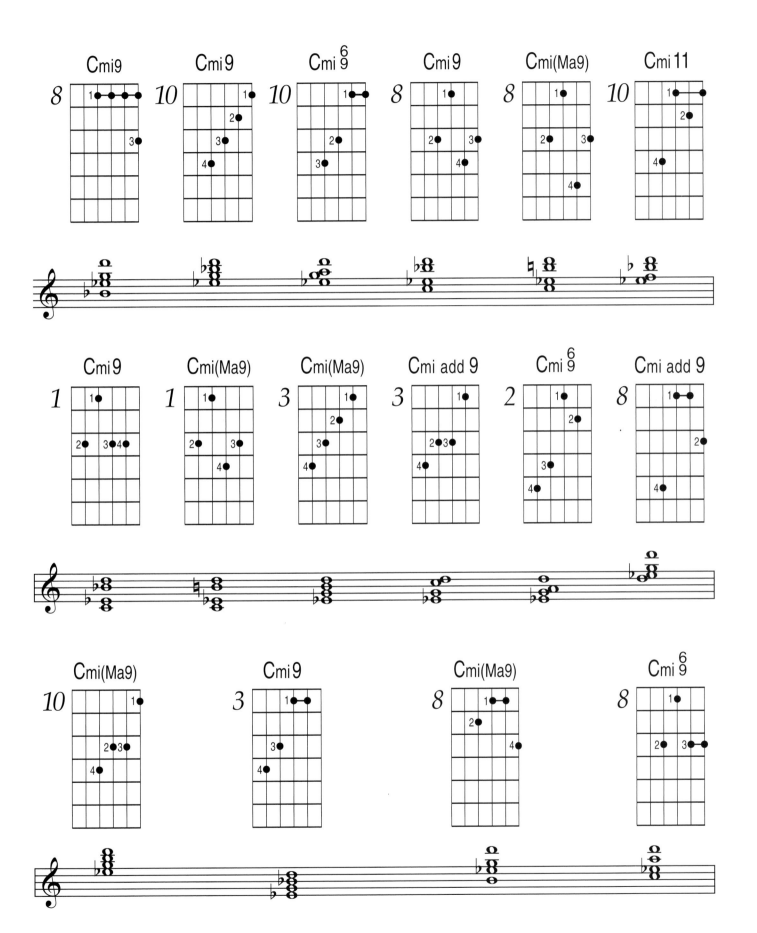

MINOR

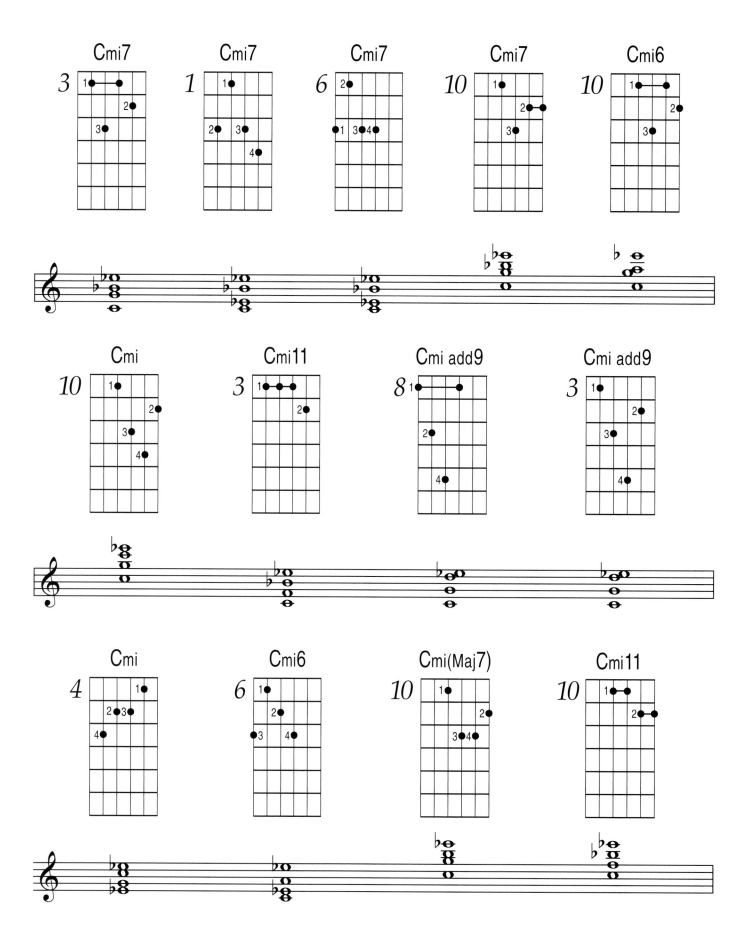

MINOR 11th

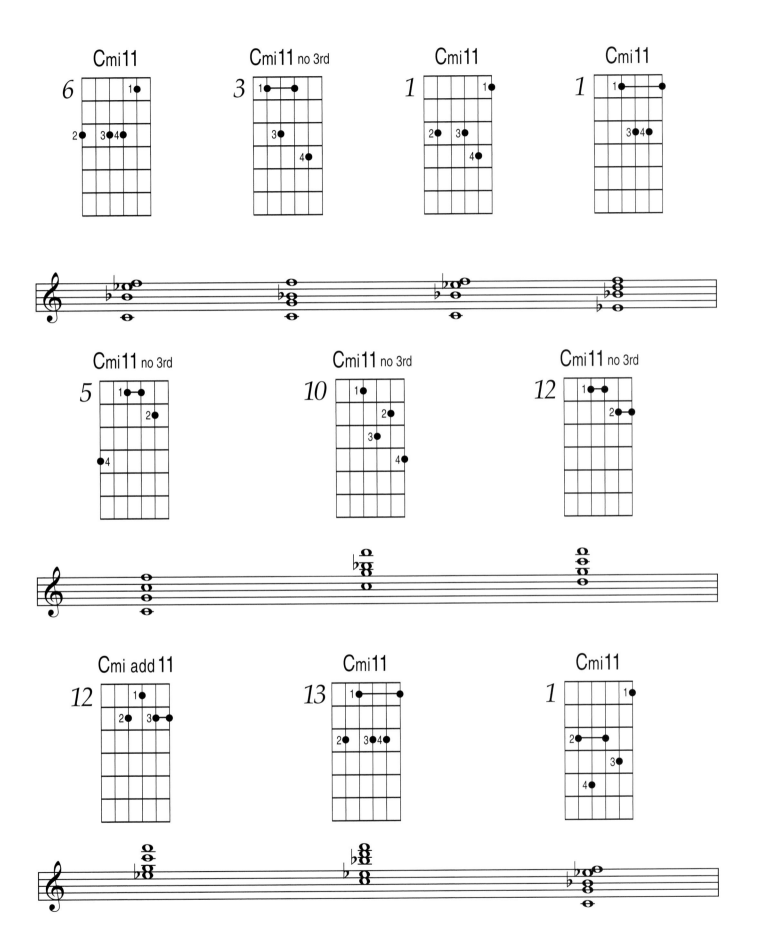

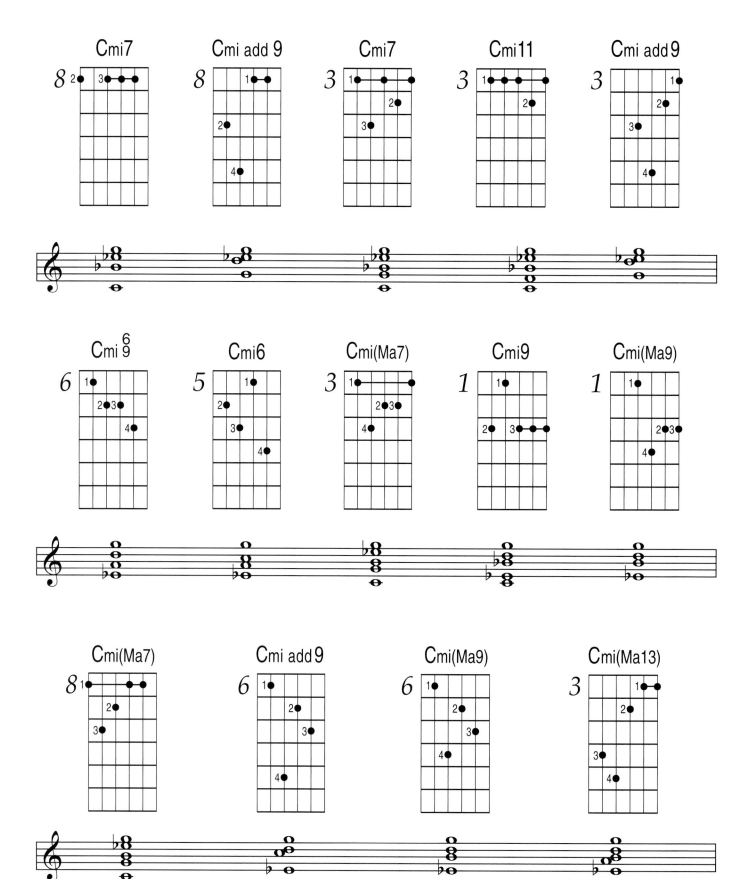

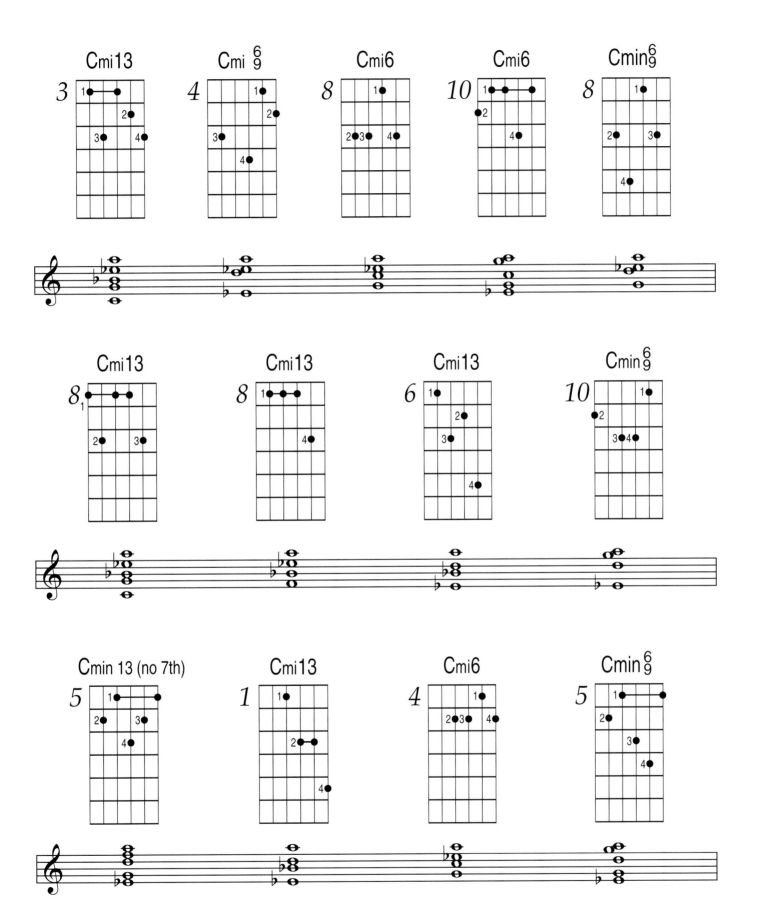

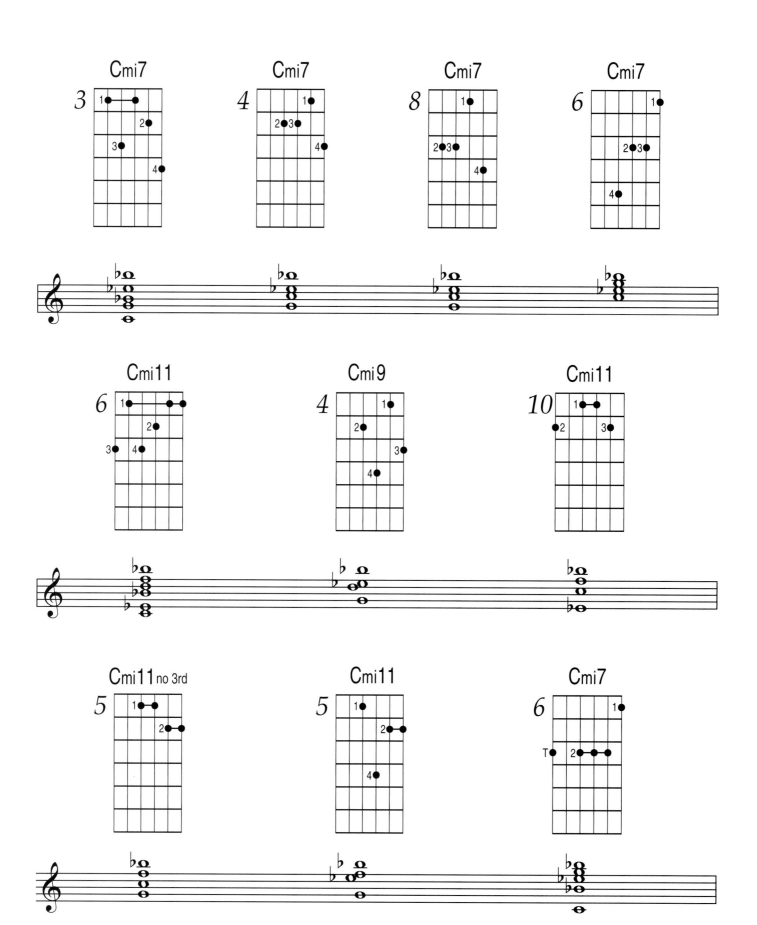

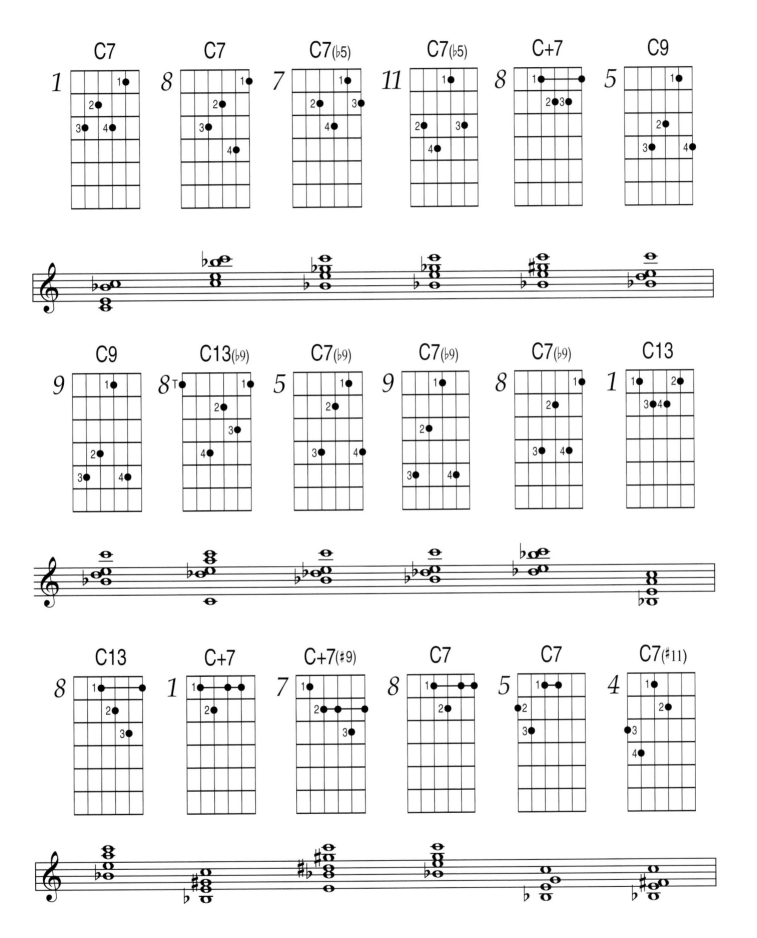

DOMINANT

b9th

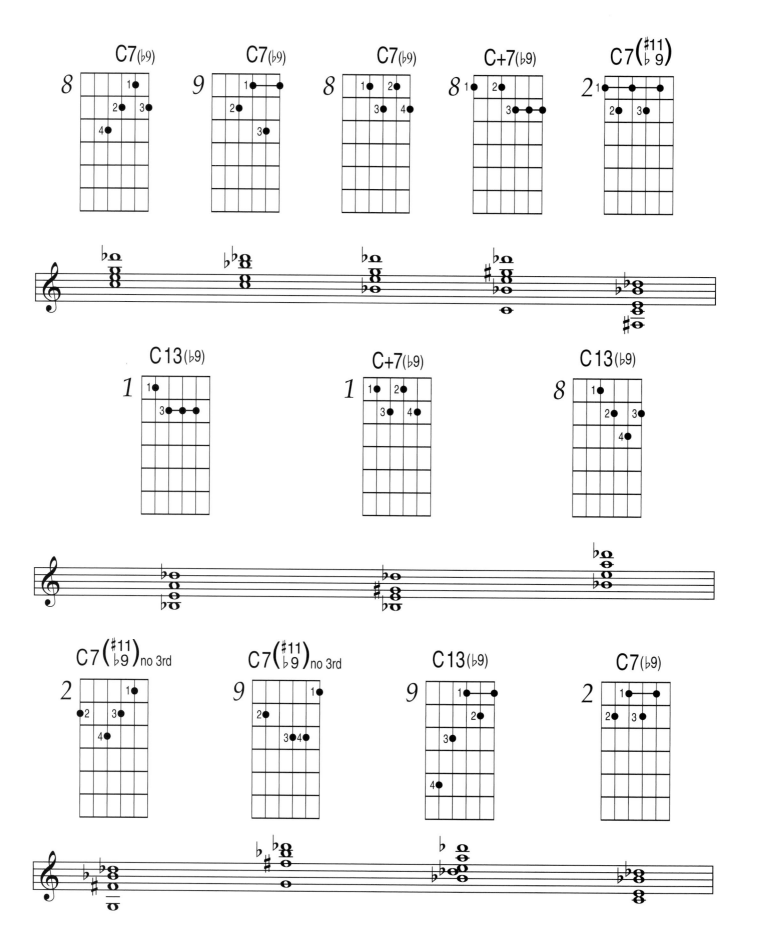

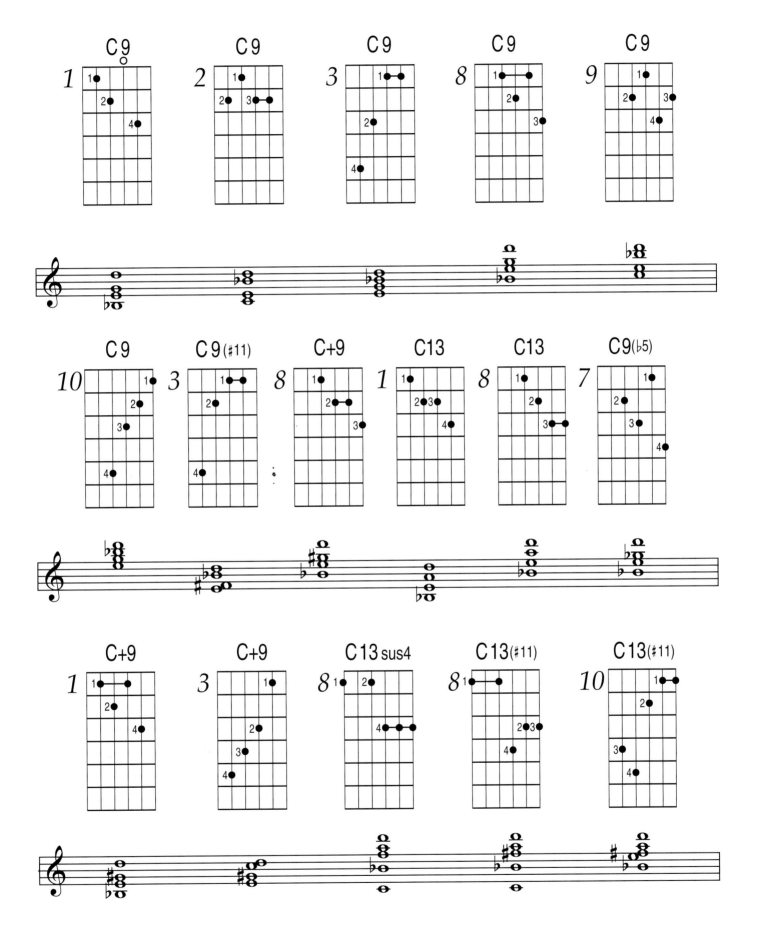

DOMINANT   #9th

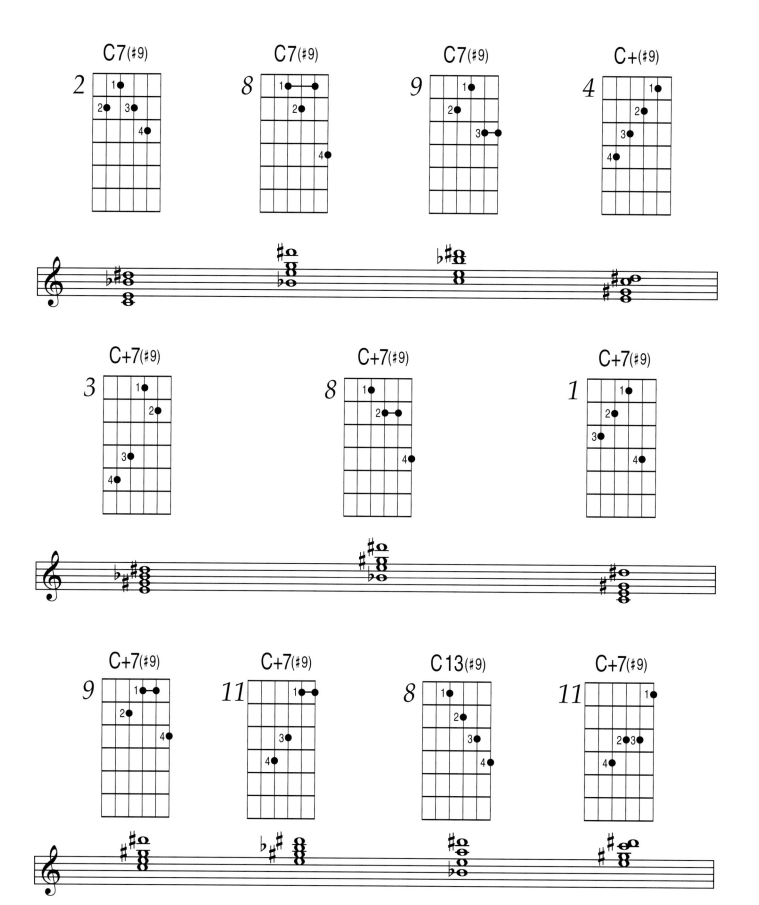

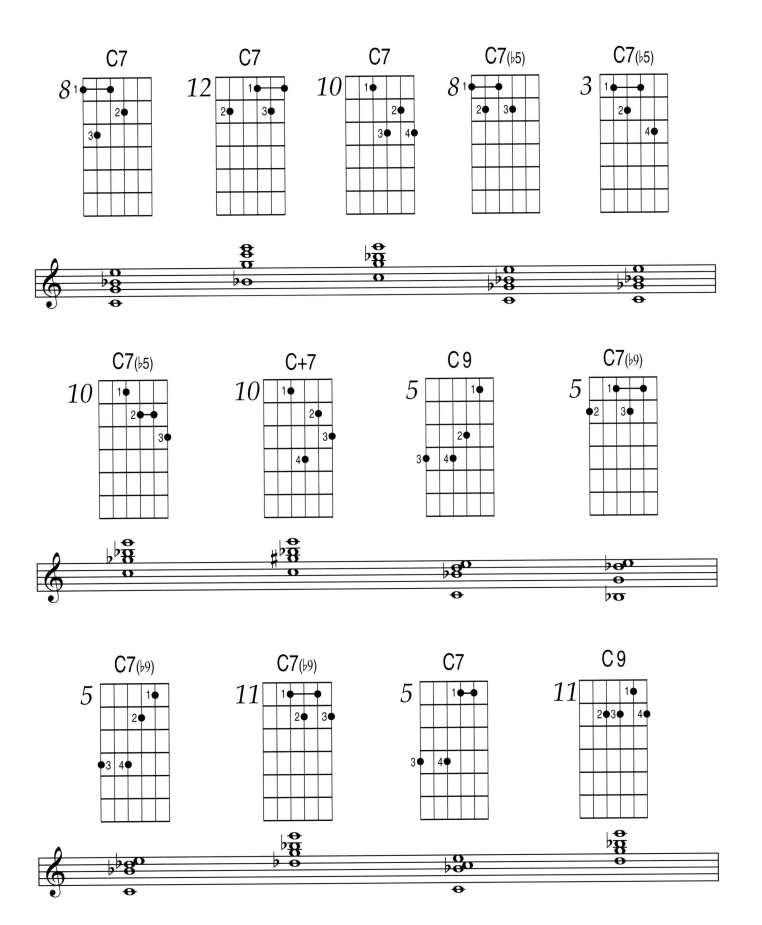

DOMINANT

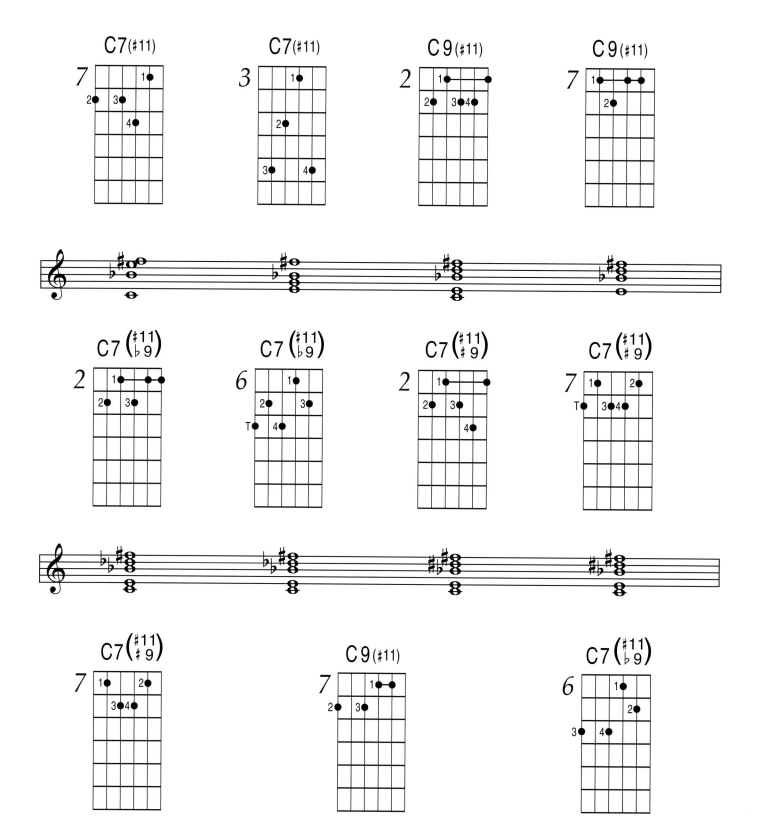

C7

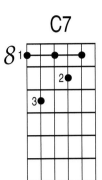

C7

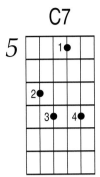

C9

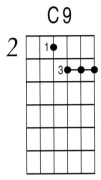

C9

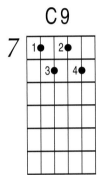

C7(♭9)

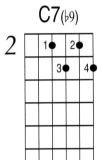

C7(♭9)

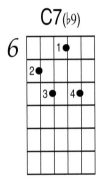

C7(♯9)

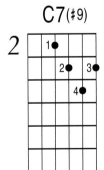

C7(♯9)

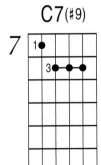

C7(♭13)

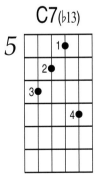

DOMINANT

C+7

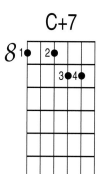

C+9

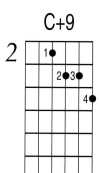

C+9

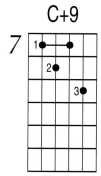

C+7(♭9)

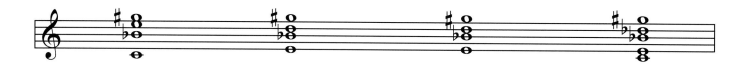

C+7(♭9)

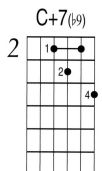

C+7(♭9)

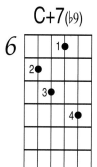

C+7(♯9)

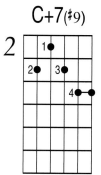

C+7(♯9)

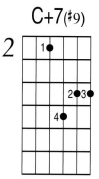

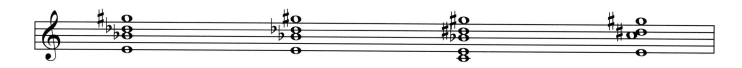

C+7(♯9)

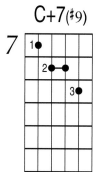

C+7(♯9)

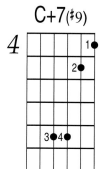

C+7(♯9)

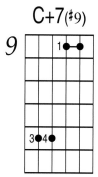

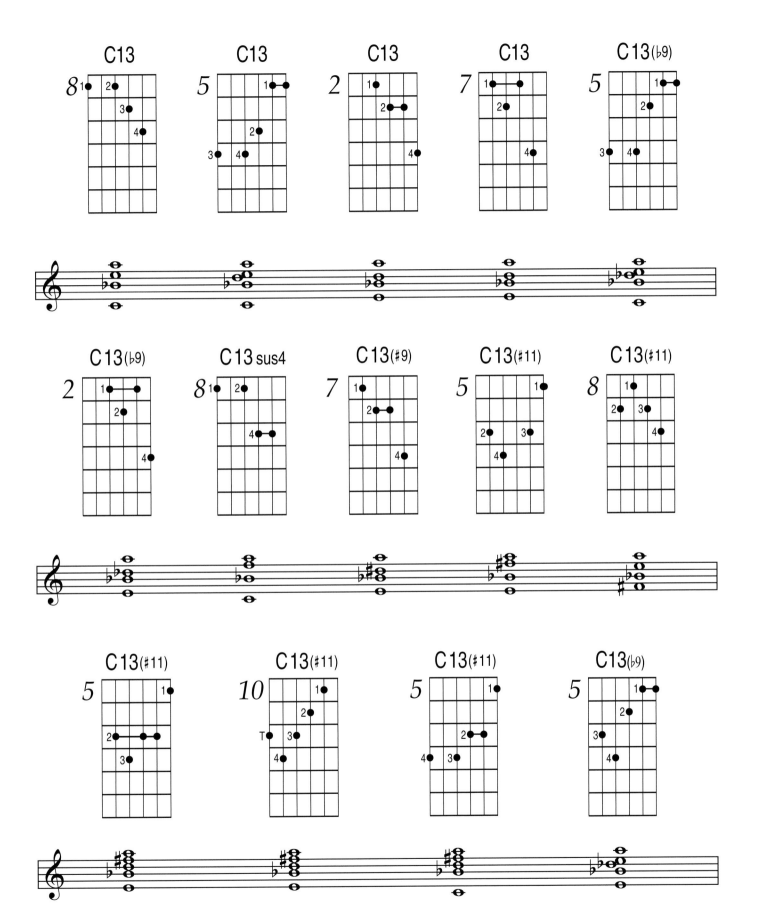

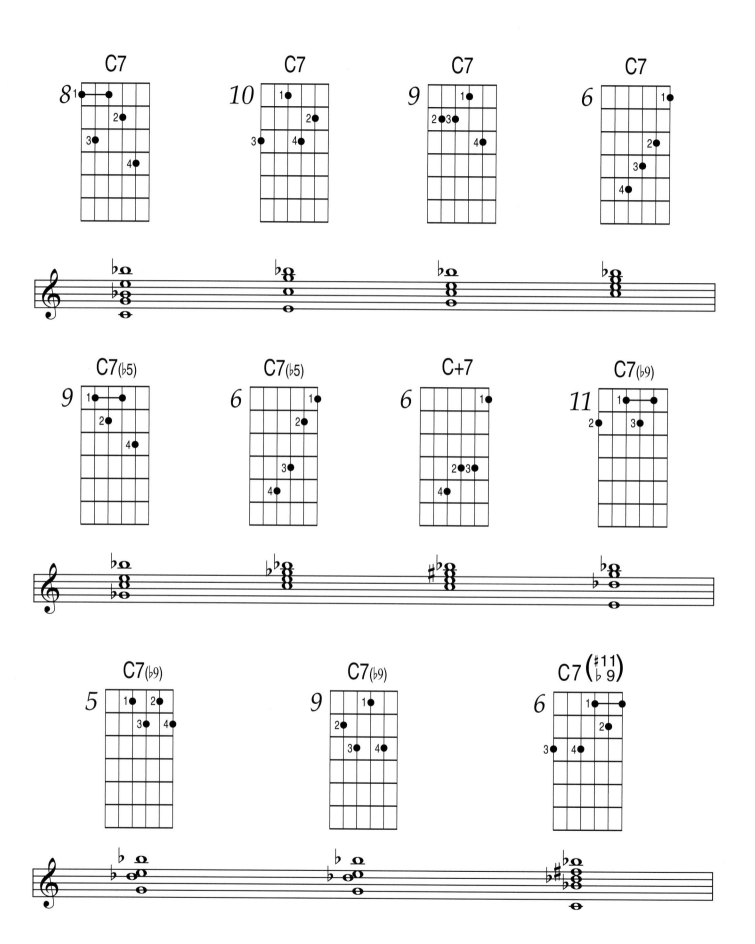

MINOR 7b5   Root

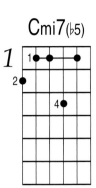

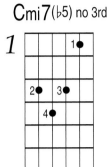

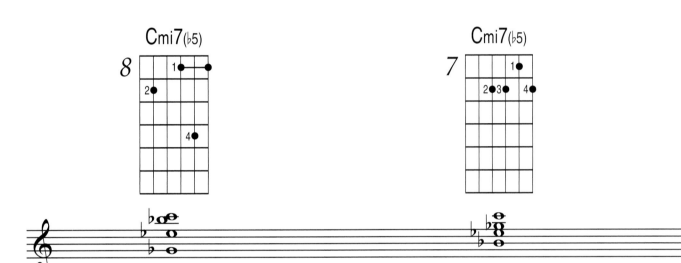

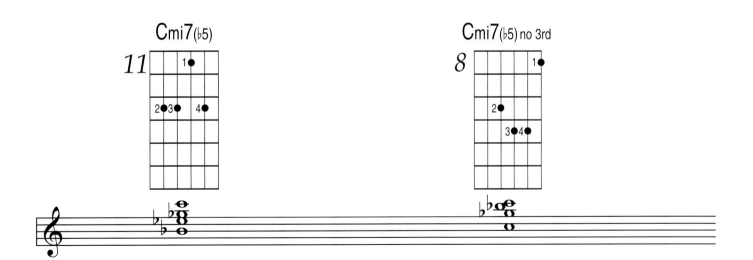

MINOR 7b5   9th

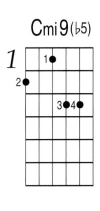
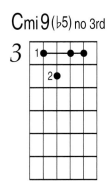
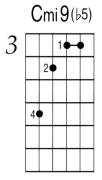

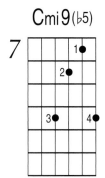
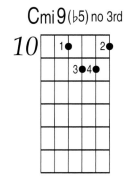

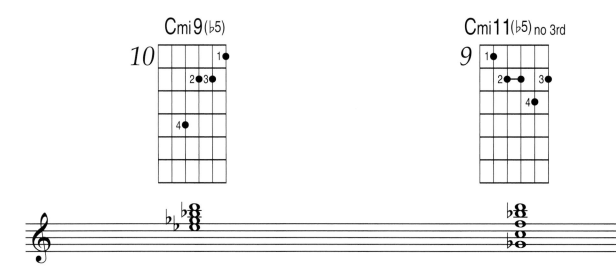

MINOR 7b5

3rd

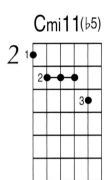

Cmi11(♭5)

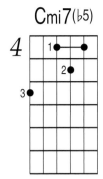

Cmi7(♭5)

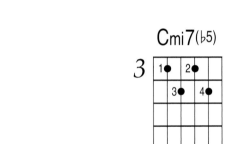

Cmi7(♭5)

Cmi7(♭5)

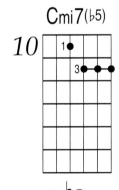

Cmi7(♭5)

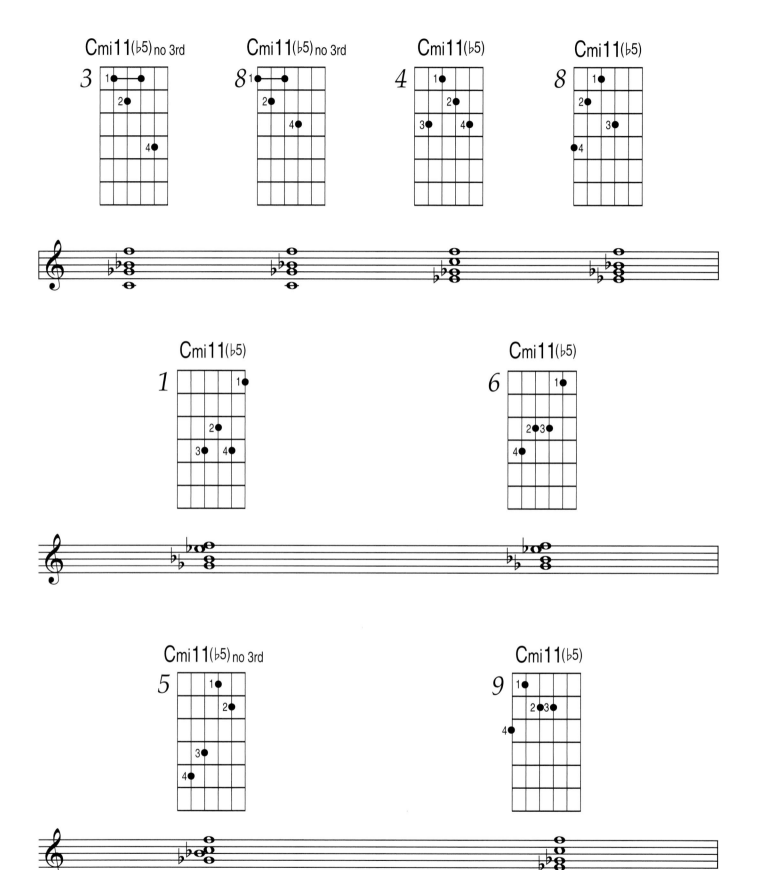

MINOR 7b5

b5th

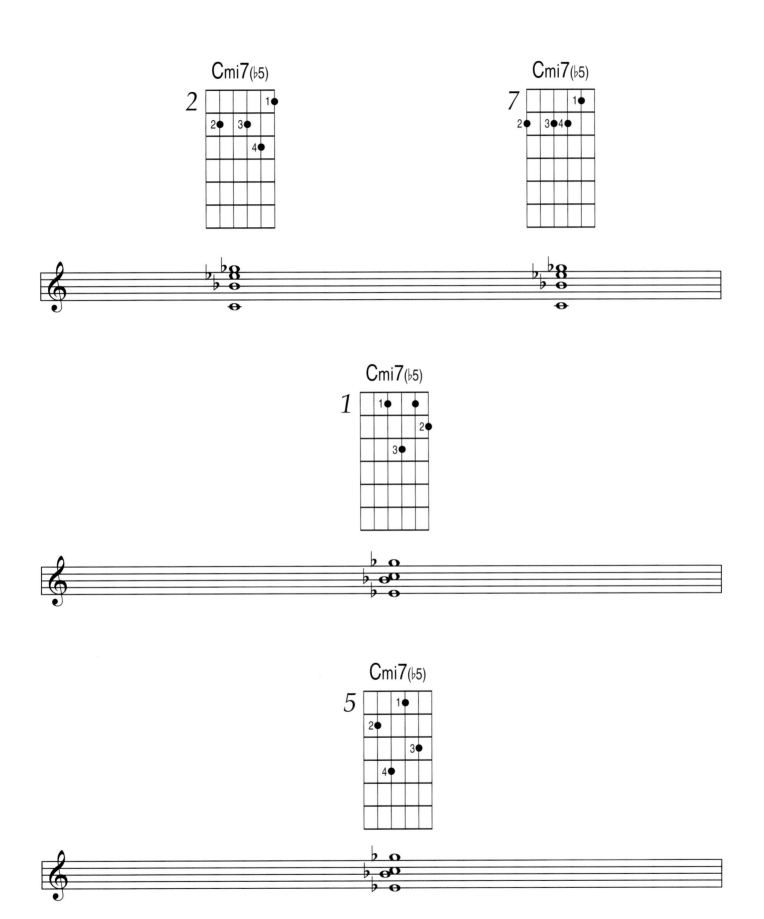

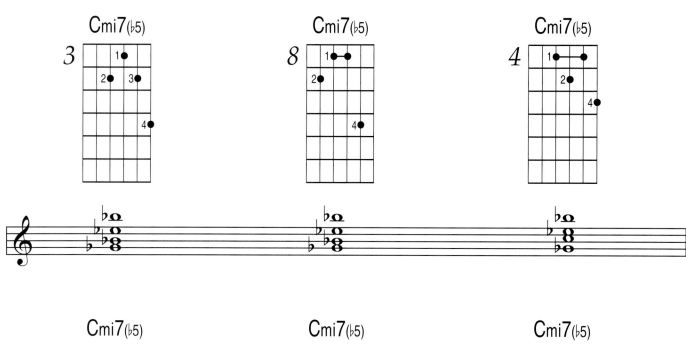

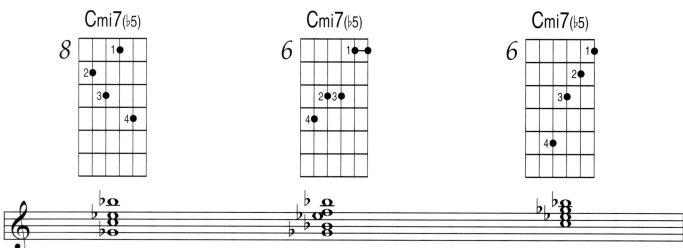

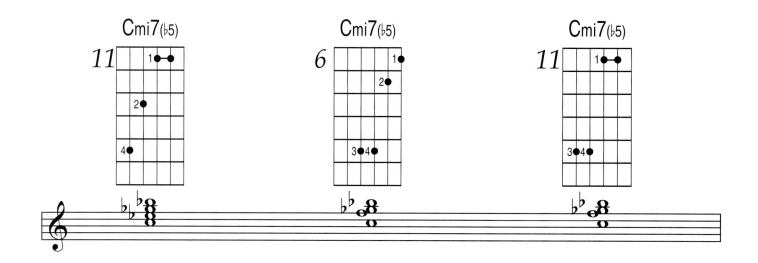

SUSPENDED

Root

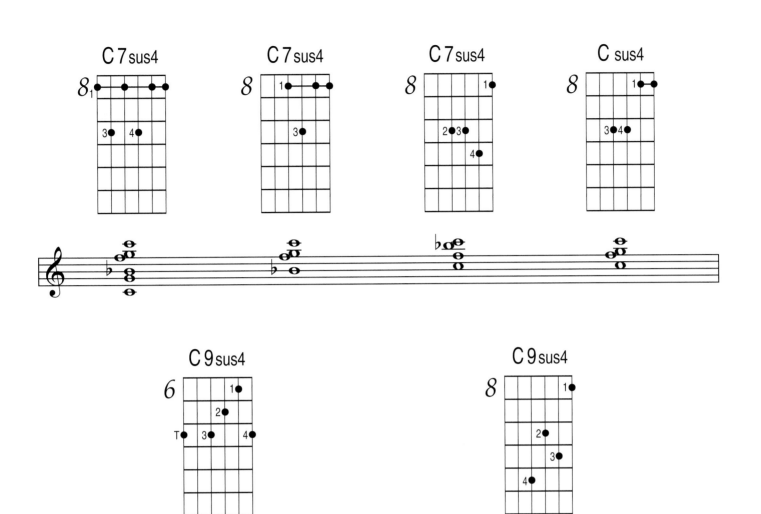

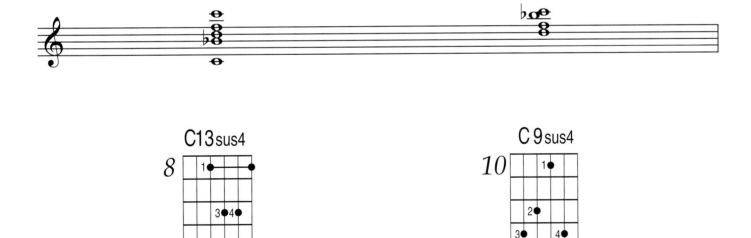

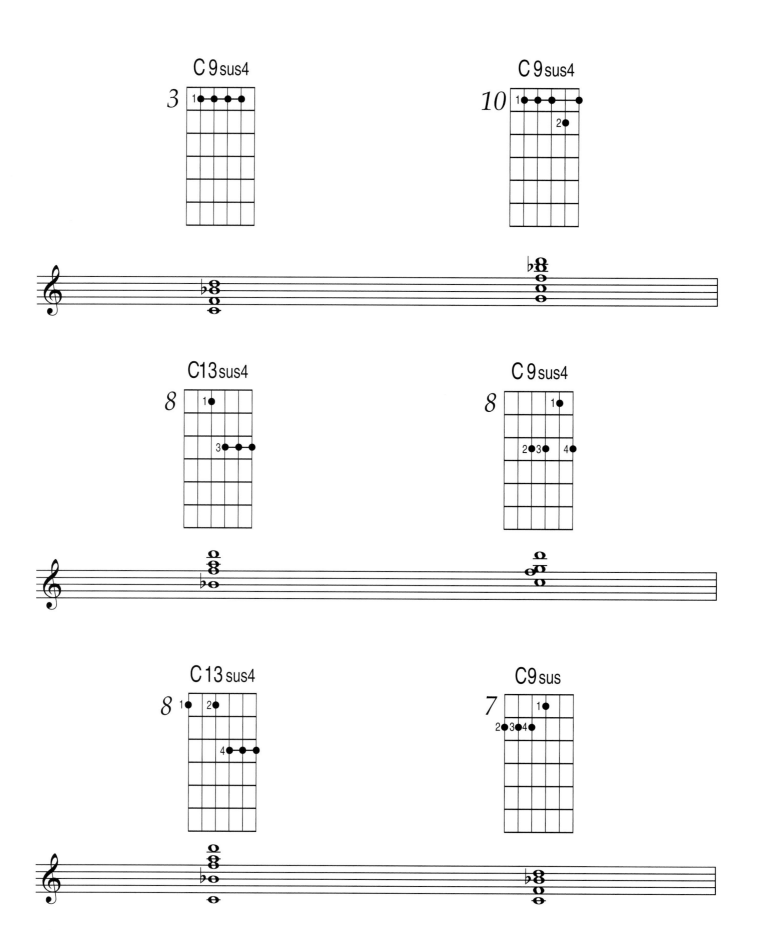

SUSPENDED 4th

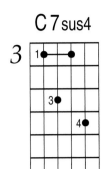

C 7 sus4

C 7 sus4

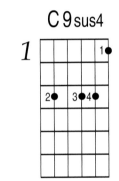

C 9 sus4

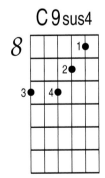

C 9 sus4

SUSPENDED

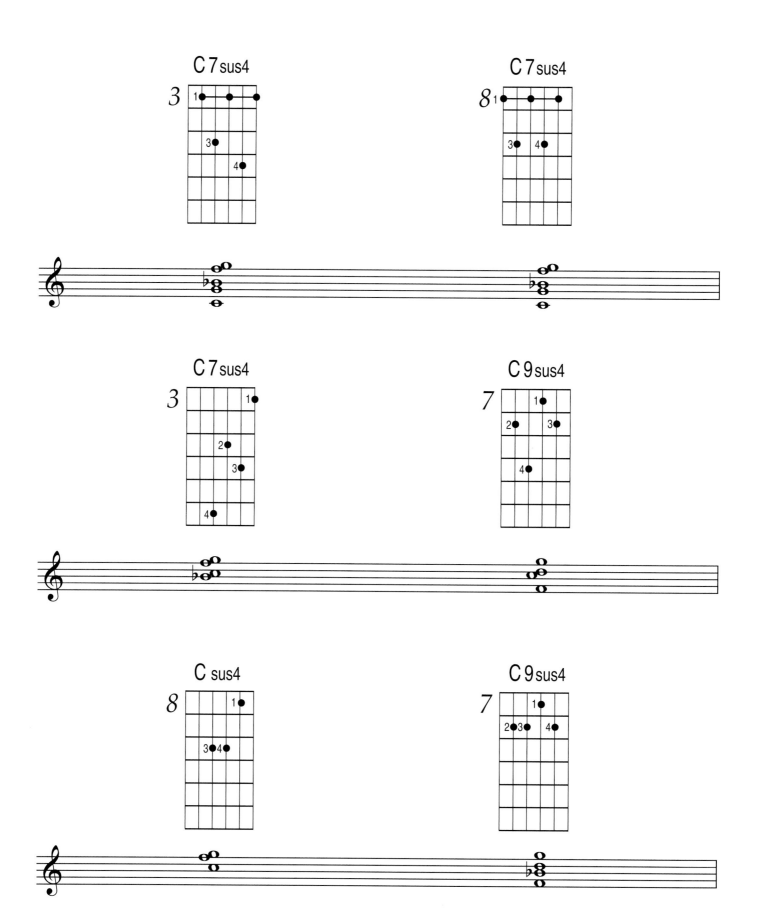

SUSPENDED

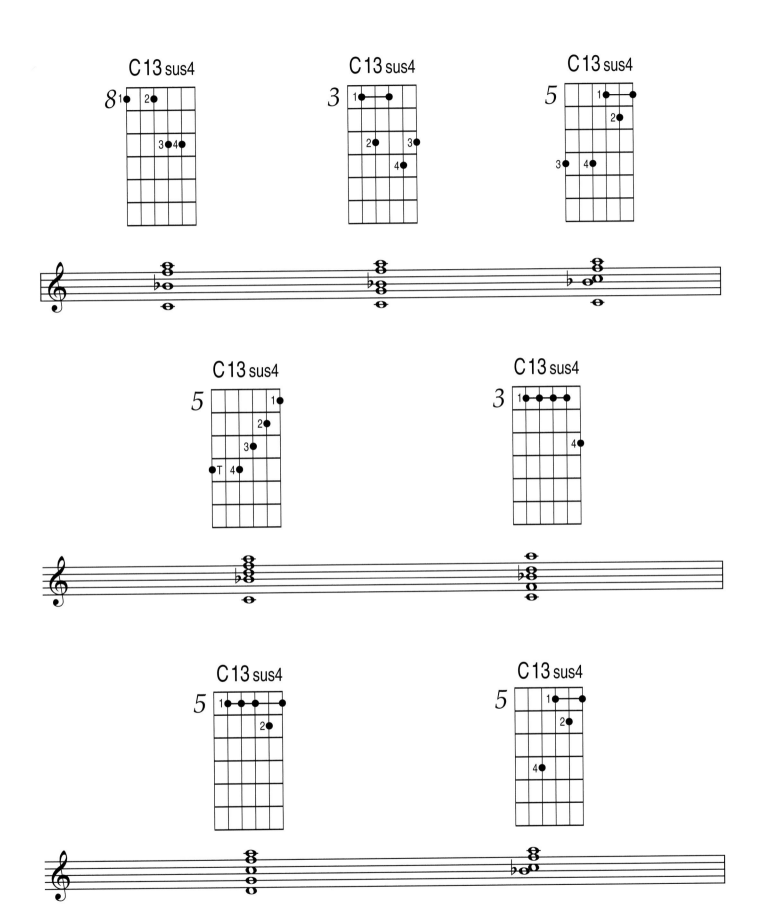

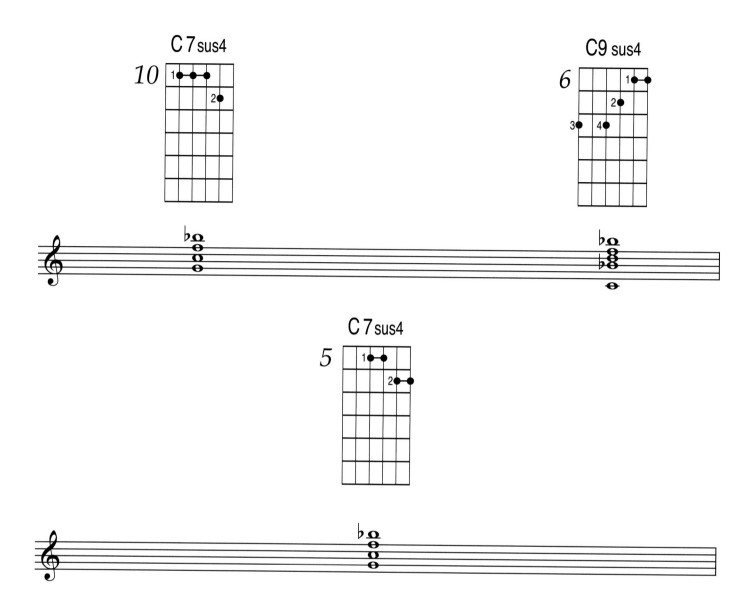

Now that you have gotten to this page, provided you didn't just skip here, you should be ready to play chords and chord progressions that are melodic, expansive, and interesting. Progressions that you could only play one way before working on this book you can now play hundreds of ways. I wish you good luck with your new chords, and may all your chord playing be melodic.

David Bloom

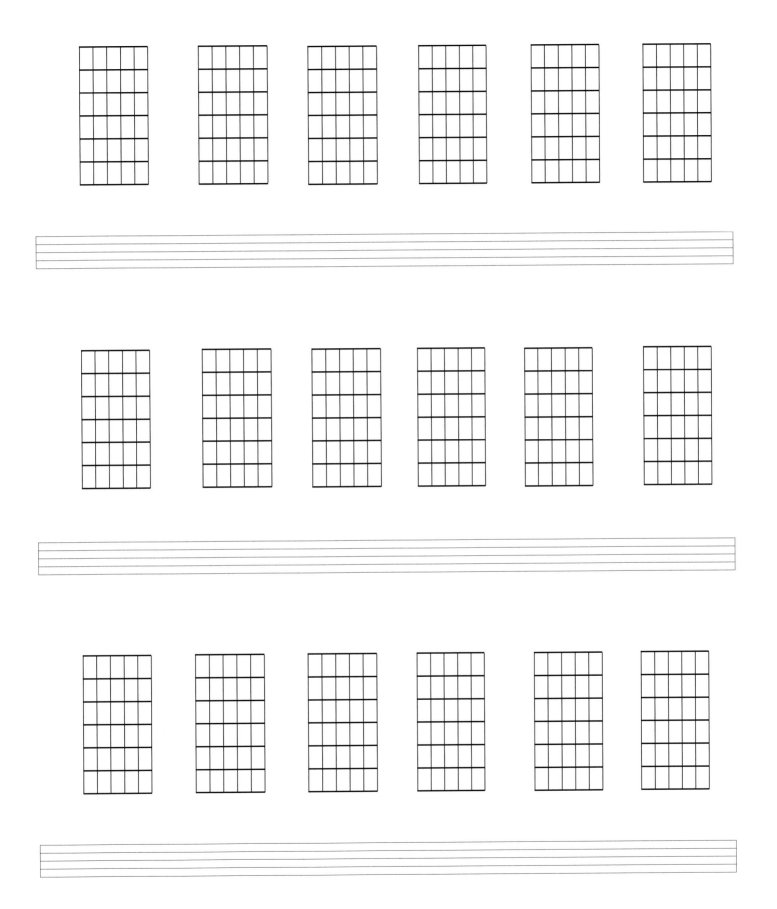

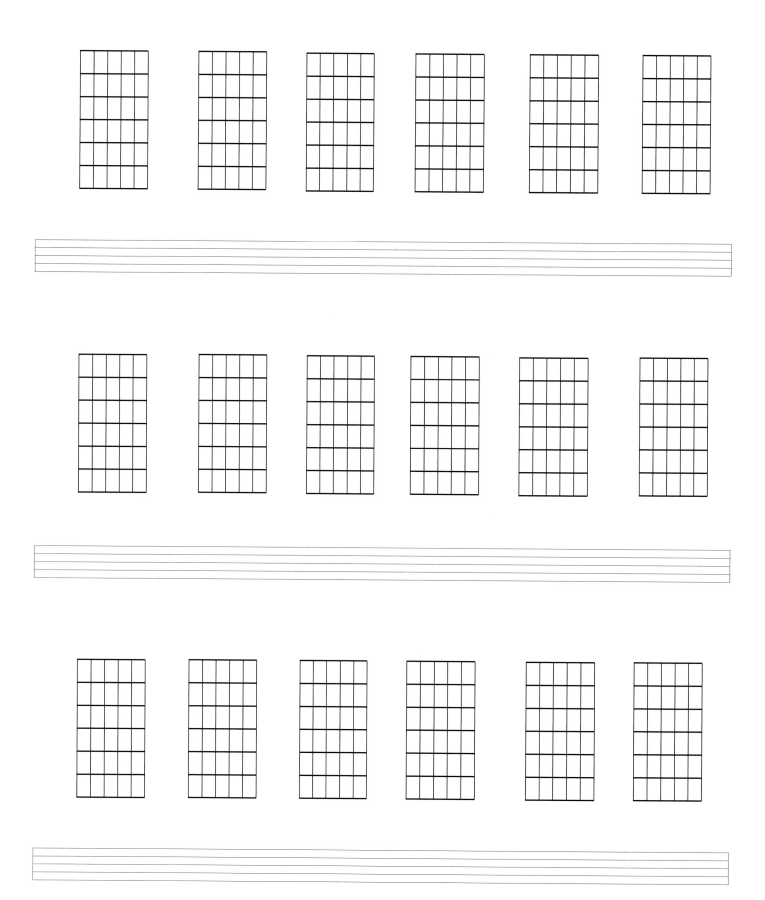

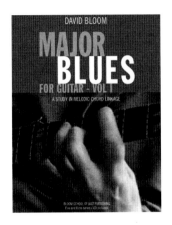
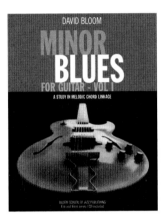
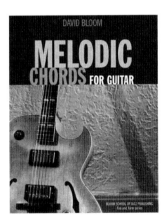

BLOOM SCHOOL OF JAZZ
218 S. Wabash, #600
Chicago, IL 60604
Phone: 312-957-9300
Fax: 312-957-0133
e-mail: dbloom1@interaccess.com

www.bloomschoolofjazz.com